The Toolbox

For Parents

Lilly J. Landikusic, LMFT
Kevin S. Lolofie, MBA

A parenting skills workbook

The Toolbox for Parents

Written by Kevin S. Lolofie & Lilly J. Landikusic

Copyright © 2010 by Kevin S. Lolofie & Lilly Landikusic.

This workbook is printed in cooperation with Empowerment Counseling Services.

Printed in the United States of America.

Please visit our website at www.empowermentcounselingservices.com.

How to use this book

There is so much information out there that sometimes it's hard to determine what works and what doesn't. If you search the internet for "How to cook a turkey," you'll find more ways to cook a turkey than there are turkeys to cook. The same goes for parenting skills.

Our aim for this book was to cut through all of the glitter and glam, all the internet and TV sensationalism, and create a menu of core parenting skills, based on the research and many years of experience in the field.

In our practice, we have seen a diverse array of families, including families with children with autism, addictions issues, conduct and oppositional defiance disorders, depression, and other special needs. We have also met families that just needed a little help getting back on track. With all families, there are a few core skills that must be used and honed and rehoned before any other issues can be addressed. There is so much information on TV and the internet - a lot of it is merely fluff to sell books - but there are really only a few skills that parents actually need.

Those are the skills that are in this book - guided solutions for you as a parent.

Skill Boxes and Scripts

There are three core skills based on the way people communicate, the way people are motivated, and the way children respond to parents as leaders of the household. There are also supporting skills that parents should pay attention to in order to help the family system as a whole function as well as possible.

These skills are easy to learn, but parents should constantly hone the skills and sub-skills - we even are constantly honing these skills for use in our own homes. What we've tried to do in this book is provide specific, practical, and guided information that provide solutions to most parenting problems.

> **What we've tried to do in this book is provide specific, practical, and guided information that provide solutions to most parenting problems.**

Throughout the book, you'll find boxes that describe the core skills and sub-skills, and some have scripted examples of proper usage. As a matter of fact, every skill that we believe is core to parenting is described in Chapter 1. The rest of the book describes those skills in detail and provides background information.

Some of the skills are scripted, because we've found that it helps to have the situation in your head before you encounter the situation with your child. Every situation will be different, but the scripts outline the basic direction of the conversation. You may want to use the script as you hone the skill, and eventually you'll find your own voice.

The First 4

You're most likely going to have to make some changes first. That doesn't mean there's something wrong with you - think of it as training. At work, training makes you a more valuable employee… at home, training will make you a more valuable parent, improving your relationships, communication, and children's behaviors.

The First 4 skills you need:

- Be able to accept feedback
- Trust the skills
- Be a role model for your child's behaviors
- Get your kids to want to follow your directions

Forward

With more than 20 years of experience working with kids and families, we have learned that much of therapy relies upon the relationships between therapist and patient, and the individual beliefs of the therapist play a large factor in the therapy process - for good or for bad.

Therapy can be counterproductive if the therapist believes in outdated or inappropriate treatment models, or uses ineffective treatment processes. Because the therapeutic process can take a lot of time before progress is recognized, ineffective therapy may not be realized for months or years, and may eventually alienate unsuccessful patients from the process entirely.

The purpose of this book is to highlight the best practices for parenting and specific tools that parents can use in everyday life and everyday situations. Based on research and experience in communicating these to our patients, we have developed these skills at the treatment model level in our own practice.

Every parent we have ever met has very personal hopes and dreams of improving their family relationships, home environment, and the lives of their children. Before you begin this process, take a moment to hold sacred your story and perseverance. If you have some control over your experience of your problems and your future relationships you hold a great degree of blessing - sometimes we forget that. I have worked with so many families in crisis, and every one of their stories is so unique and remarkable.

Most of our families have become seriously concerned with escalating problems with their children. They are worried about their future, their relationships, their abilities to depend on themselves and find peace and happiness into their adulthoods. What has brought you to this point?

Contents

Skills in The Parenting Toolbox

Simplify

Topics in this chapter

The Toolbox for Parents

Step 1 - Jump right in!

The Calm Tone

Effective Reinforcement

Parenting Empowerment

Discipline

Other important skills for parents

Every parent needs a toolbox

Simplify

- This first chapter outlines all of the skills in the book, and the rest of the book explains how to use them
- Let's simplify good parenting techniques and then practice a few skills at a time
- You have to be willing to change first, before you can expect your child to change
    - Be able to accept feedback
    - Stick to the skills
    - Be a role model
    - Get your kids to WANT to follow you
- Reward good behaviors, and correct wrong behaviors by teaching, not punishing
- The Top 3 Parenting Skills are The Calm Tone, Effective Reinforcement, and Parenting Empowerment

The Toolbox for Parents

Most parents know that being a good parent is more than loving your child. Oftentimes, parents are so focused on the important daily functions – let's face it, there are so many things to do and so little time – that it can be difficult to problem-solve the behaviors that we'd like to change in our children.

Confusing things even more are all of the "professionals" in the media that offer advice as "universal truths," even though all the advice is often conflicting and usually doesn't take into account our busy daily lives. In this book, we have taken the best research and simplified everything to enable parents to integrate actual skills into daily life. The most simplified way to describe our skill set is this:

Reward + Teach = Happy
good behavior   don't punish   Parenting

This book is for parents who are looking for skills that will effectively shape their child's behaviors. This workbook isn't presenting any new information – we're probably telling you what you already know. **This book is merely a toolbox to help you simplify, hone, and renew your skills by highlighting the important skills that are often forgotten** during our busy daily lives.

Whether we like it or not, our children generally become adults with the behaviors that we taught them. The core parenting skills are not the behaviors that we think are important to teach to children, based on our beliefs; they are tools for teaching your children the behaviors that you value. Also, the Big 3 Parenting Skills can improve a child's school and relationship successes, while preventing the behaviors from getting so bad that they cause health, addictions, and legal problems.

The first chapter of this book will summarize all of the skills that are required in order to implement the Parenting Toolbox. The rest of the book will go into further detail on how to appropriately use the skills, as well as background information on the skills. **You have to give 100% to changing yourself before you can expect any change in your child.**

By picking this book off the shelf, you've shown that you're looking for help with parenting skills, and being able to accept feedback and change is the first step. Although you're trying to affect your child's behavior, you will be doing most of the work throughout this process. There are skills that you will probably have to teach to your child, but behavior modification mostly involves implementing a reward system, while changing negative communication and relationship habits.

Step 1 – Jump right in!

This workbook is designed for parents – you have to be willing to learn new skills first, and then trust that these skills work. Use the skills over a four week period – stick to your guns – and you will see changes that will last a long time.

> **The First 4 skills you need:**
> - **Be able to accept feedback**
> - **Trust the skills**
> - **Be a role model for your child**
> - **Get your kids to WANT to follow your directions**

Also, you have to role model behaviors for your child. Some people blame the media, the child's peers, professional athletes, and politicians for being bad role models for children. In those cases, those external factors are being given way too much power, power that the parent should be retaining to role model behaviors. **You control what your child learns!**

We should also say that this is a process. Learning the skills is a process, mastering the skills is a process, and managing your child's behaviors is a process. And the process takes time… life is a marathon, not a sprint. Once you learn the language, however, the process will get easier, because you will begin to respond to all situations using the same basic skills.

The Big 3 Parenting Skills

	The Calm Tone	Effective Reinforcement	Parenting Empowerment
Result	Improves communication skills; creates healthy relationships; fosters school and career achievement; protects personal values and goals	Gives the child a sense of control over rewards; teaches how the world really works – based on rewards and consequences; teaches the child to strive for success in school, work, and relationships	Empowers the child to make her own decisions; develops an internal locus of control; improves school success; provides impulse control through delayed gratification; teaches decision-making
Reduces risk factors	Decreases conflict in the home and school; decreases resentment when someone crosses your boundaries; prevents mixed signals; or feeling like "mom is always mad"	Reduces the need for punishment; reduces parent stress; reduces the use of negative communication skills that can affect the child's self concept	Reduces: • Delinquency • Alcohol & drug use • Oppositional Defiance • Behavioral problems

This book will also discuss other skills that are important in shaping your child's lifestyle, both in and outside of the home.

Know your values

Your child will learn the values that you teach or role model. If you role model honesty, your child will learn honesty. If you role model making excuses, your child will learn to make excuses. Values can be anything important to you, including people, places, things, and ideas, such as honesty and freedom. What values are in your value set - your list of Top 25 values?

Your personal value set: first brainstorm your values, and write them in the blanks. Once you've written down all of the values you can think of, go back and rank them.

Rank	Value name	Rank	Value name	Rank	Value name
—	_____	—	_____	—	_____
—	_____	—	_____	—	_____
—	_____	—	_____	—	_____
—	_____	—	_____	—	_____
—	_____	—	_____	—	_____
—	_____	—	_____	—	_____
—	_____	—	_____	—	_____
—	_____	—	_____	—	_____
—	_____				

The Calm Tone

The Calm Tone

- Use a quiet, normal tone of voice, whether the child is calm and playing or tantrumming and screaming.

- Check your non-verbal style, especially your posture, gestures, and facial expressions, to determine if they are affecting your ability to teach your child important skills.

- If you're not sure if you may be having problems with your other non-verbals, remember this simple rule: continue doing what you were doing before the behavior, act as if the behavior didn't affect you at all.

- The 2 Faces of Parenting:
  - Use the HAPPY FACE when reinforcing a good behavior
  - Use the POKER FACE when you see an unwanted behavior

- Wait for a break in the behavior, prepare a statement of praise, and then reinforce the break:
  "I'm so glad you're going to stop yelling, whenever you feel like talking about what's going on, just let me know."
  "I'm so glad you're not whining anymore, because I can't understand what you want when you're whining. We can talk now, if you want."

- **During a problem-behavior situation, teach The Calm Tone skill first.** Teaching communication skills is critical for the other skills to work! When a child is doing a problem behavior that is preventing communication – yelling, crying, acting aggressively, whining, running around, ignoring – don't worry about anything else at the moment.

Managing your household also becomes easier when you create an environment where your child WANTS to follow your directions. Imagine going to a job where your boss is constantly yelling or criticizing you, doesn't follow his own values, and spanks you or punishes you when you do something wrong. The first skill that you have to learn is The Calm Tone.

Getting your kids to WANT to follow your directions does not mean that you have to bribe them with candy, toys, or other things. The Calm Tone sets up the tone of the way the family communicates. As the child learns the tone of communications, then the focus will turn to what is being communicated.

The bottom line for this first skill is that the tone of the conversation is just as important as the content of the communication, and it is easy for adults to forget that a loud tone can be perceived by a child as aggressive, which equates to fear, resentment, and possibly anger.

Using a Calm Tone is the best way to decrease conflict. No matter how high the child is trying to increase the level of conflict, the parent should always show Calm Tone. In fact, the parent should become even calmer as the child escalates.

Disengaging

1. Let the child know that you're going to disengage.
2. Walk away and find something else to do.
3. When the child is calm, reinforce her calming down.
4. Teach the healthy communication skills. (P.23)
5. Teach other skills only after "Calm Tone" has been resolved

Disengaging is a sub-skill of The Calm Tone, that teaches the child to communicate using healthy skills, or don't communicate at all until he is able to do so calmly.

We've seen a lot of parents who just can't disengage, which creates a cycle of conflict. The child learns that engaging in the conflict is part of communication, which will affect future relationships, school progress, and work opportunities. **If the goal is to teach healthy communication skills to create good relationship skills and work ethic,** the parent has to role model the skill of disengaging.

The two faces of parenting

The happy face is just what it sounds like – happy. Smiling, excitement in the eyes, animated facial expressions – all show the emotion of being happy. People love being happy, and love being around other people who are happy, and the same is true for children. Children are more likely to follow the parent, learn from the parent, and comply with the parent's rules and values, if they are happy with the parent.

The poker face is the other face that parents can use, and has no expression. Poker players watch their opponents, looking for changes in verbal and non-verbal communication as indicators of thoughts and emotions. In parenting, having no facial expression shows the child that the problem behavior will not affect the outcome of the situation, will not get the child what he wants, and that he should try a different approach to getting what he wants. **You're actually ignoring the unwanted behavior, and waiting for the wanted behavior with a prepared reward or praise.**

Body Language

- **Posturing** is the way a person stands in relation to the other person in the conversation. A range of emotions could be expressed in the way a person postures her body. Someone could perceive aggression if the posture is threatening, such as being bent over the other person, or standing in someone's personal space. Standing close to someone could also indicate affection or a feeling of closeness.

- **Gestures** include the motions made with the hands and arms, including non-motion, such as folding the arms across the chest or clutching a door frame. Gestures can present warmth, openness, and nurturing, such as with a hug or open arms. They could also present the opposite, with the arms folded across the chest, or holding the arm out to distance the other person.

- **Facial expressions** are probably the most transparent of the non-verbal styles, and can include the entire range of emotions expressed by blinking eyes, frowning, smiling, or any other facial contortion. It is here that we will discuss the two faces of parenting: the happy face and the poker face.

Passive – "Walked all over"

- Avoids conflict at all costs, by allowing others to have their way
- Does not assert own wants and needs
- Agrees to everything every time
- Creates Lose-Win outcomes
- May often feel victimized
- Feels that speaking up will lead to rejection by others
- May not know own needs, assumes the values and goals of others
- Usually indicates lower self esteem
- Learned from parent or abuse
- May feel like the strength of the relationship is more important than the conflict
- Own needs are not met, may not have own needs or values
- May enter relationships with others who will take advantage of passivity
- Always backs down from conflict

Aggressive – "The Bully"

- Tone and non-verbals may often be threatening to others
- Intentional disregard for others' feelings and needs, no empathy
- Meets own needs by intimidating and controlling others
- Creates Win-Lose outcomes
- Learned in childhood that aggression and violence are the only ways for communicating
- Usually indicates family history of violence
- Usually indicates lower self esteem, stemming from a sense of inadequacy in one or more areas of life
- Relationships are usually less important than power and control, most relationships will fail
- May enter relationships with others who will be submissive

Passive-Aggressive – "Hidden Aggression"

- Combines the Passive and Aggressive styles of communication:
- Wants to be aggressive, but usually fears rejection
- Uses inappropriate sarcasm, procrastination, sabotage, and other HIDDEN behaviors in an attempt to meet needs
- Often creates Lose-Lose or Lose-Win outcomes
- Hidden agendas undermine relationships
- May be able to gain the trust of others, but eventually loses trust because of ulterior motives
- May often feel victimized, until acting out through impulse behaviors
- Likely learned behaviors and communication from parents – parent was either passive, aggressive or passive-aggressive

Assertive – "Direct with Respect"

- Asserts wants, needs, values in a direct and open manner
- Uses "I want," "I need," or "I feel" statements
- Ex. "I want our family to communicate better." "We need to clean the house."
- Able to accept rejection, can accept "no" for an answer
- Creates Win-Win outcomes
- Develops relationships based on open communication
- Respects the needs and values of others
- Gains trust and respect from others
- Often meets needs, knows how to ask for help, and problem-solves effectively
- Usually maintains own boundaries, and respects the boundaries of others

The most effective way to communicate!

Accepting "NO" for an answer

Being able to accept "NO" for an answer is a very important skill, and most people don't realize that it's a skill. How do you react when someone tells you "NO"? **This table shows how people using the 4 different styles of communication react to being told "NO."**

Style	Reaction
Passive	People who are passive are usually okay when they are told "NO," and probably won't pursue the matter any further. Passive people are usually unlikely to assert their own wants, needs, and values, and will go along with what others tell them to do.
Aggressive	Aggressive people may become angry when told "NO," and will likely use force, threats, intimidation, or other control tactics to press the issue. They will usually continue until they find an "out," a way to end the conflict without "losing face."
Pass-Aggr	Passive-Aggressive people will usually use sarcasm, hidden aggression, or make "snide remarks," when told "NO." These people **want** to meet their wants, needs, and values, but are scared to assert themselves, for fear of rejection.
Assertive	The assertive person remains calm and polite, and may even ask, "Is there any way we can make this work for both of us?" This person begins the problem-solving process when told "NO," but is also able to say, "Well, thank you for your time," and then walk away okay.

It is easy to see how the assertive style is the most effective for maintaining healthy boundaries. Being able to accept "NO" for an answer is the same as being able to respect the boundaries that other people create for themselves. We have to respect other people's boundaries, if we expect other people to respect our boundaries.

There is a way to practice the skill of accepting "NO" for an answer in an assertive manner:

1.   **Assertive statement:** Ask for what you want. Be polite and respectful, but be direct. "I need to borrow the car, because some of my friends are going to the basketball game."
   "NO"

2.   **Feeling statement:** I feel _____, BECAUSE I _____ _____. I would like to _____.
   "NO"

3.   **Thankful statement:** Be appreciative of the things you have. Keep the relationship open for future needs. "Well, thanks anyway, I appreciate you listening, and I respect your decision."

Effective Reinforcement

Shaping behaviors

The stimulus or situation affects the child's attitude in that brief moment in time. The situation can change the attitude – bad or good – or the attitude can stay the same. The attitude – thoughts, emotions, and physical reaction – then affect the behavior, which in turn causes the parent to react. In the future, anytime the child perceives a similar stimulus or situation, she will use what she learned from prior situations to guide her behavior.

This is the Behavior Shaping Model:

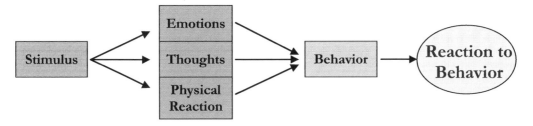

Usually, a negative consequence will cause a person to stop or change the behavior the next time he is in that same situation.

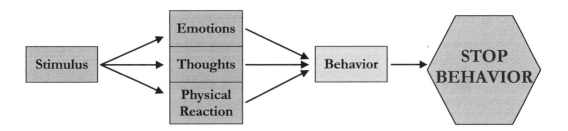

When we receive a positive outcome during a situation, we are more likely to use that successful behavior every time we are in the same situation. Over time, we will continue to reproduce that behavior, each time our thoughts including the memory of previous successful outcomes.

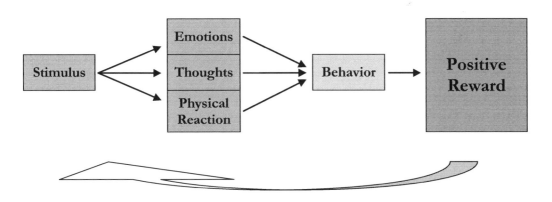

This process of perceived rewards works for healthy and unhealthy behaviors. For example, a teenager may go to a party, use alcohol to excess, and not perceive any immediate negative consequences, and will therefore be more likely to repeat that behavior in the future. Some things may take longer than others before a consequence is received, and the child may not be able to fully comprehend your instructions when the behavior is committed. It is necessary to master The Calm Tone and effective communication skills, and then develop new reward mechanisms to replace the perceived rewards from the unhealthy behaviors.

The 3 P's of Effective Reinforcement

1. **Plan: develop a plan based on the behaviors that you want to your child to do more often**
   a. **Based on your value set – determine what values you want to work on with your child**
      - Be specific – what exactly are you trying to change?
      - Fight the good fight – change the important things first
      - If you feel overwhelmed with the changes that you want to make, focus on the most important ones first
      - Calm Tone should be first – to eliminate the stresses of arguments, whining, begging, and crying
      - Empowerment is important for the child's growth
   b. **Be realistic**
      - Consider your child's age, level of understanding, cognitive abilities, vocabulary limitations
      - Set small goals first to build confidence
      - Make goals achievable and help your child succeed, failure will stop the change process
   c. **Write things down, keep things simple**

2. **Prepare: prepare your reward and how you are going to present it**
   a. **Rewards don't have to be tangible, Strategic Praise is the best reward in any situation**
   b. **Be specific**
      - What can you use to reward the child?
      - What will the child value?
      - How will you communicate that to the child?
      - Be realistic – don't promise anything you can't give
   c. **Commit the entire family**
      - Make sure your significant other is on board
      - Teach older siblings to help you reinforce wanted behaviors in younger children
      - Communicate your goals to your family
      - Take precautions not to reward the wrong behaviors

3. **Patience**
   - Be patient, wait for the behavior, wait for the change
   - When you see the behavior: reward, reward, reward
   - If you don't see the behavior: teach, teach, teach
   - Use a Calm Tone when teaching, and be assertive with your needs
   - Use "I need," "I want," or "I feel" statements
   - Practice the wanted behavior with your child
   - Connect the behavior to the bigger picture

The most effective reward: Strategic Praise

Strategic Praise has two qualities that anchor it as the most effective reward and create long-lasting relationship patterns: affection and quality one-on-one time. These aspects of Strategic Praise raise it to a level of significant positive relationship building, where the child can feel the connection of a caring relationship through affection and valued one-on-one time.

Affection is characterized by loving remarks, appropriate touching, and conversations that are exclusive to the parent and child. Affection expresses care, warmth, and love, and is the best way to build the relationship and sidestep problems. The more warmth and love that is felt in the relationship, the more the child is willing to do whatever the parent expects.

Strategic Praise

- Use a Calm Tone and positive statements
- Timing is everything – try to praise as soon as you see the good behavior
- Short, sweet, and to the point – remember that praise is a reward, and a reward is supposed to be enjoyable

That's great that you _____, I'm so happy that you did that! I need you to do that more often, okay? It's important, because _____.

The last part of that Strategic Praise statement is where the parent has to connect the behavior to the bigger picture. This helps the child begin to use critical thinking skills to engage in abstract thought.

Your job is to create an environment where your child will want to follow your instructions, not out of fear, but out of respect.

The rewards don't matter if your child won't listen to you in the first place. **The easiest way to turn off your child is to lecture, argue, yell, physically discipline, or fail to use affection and quality time.**

The use of affection and quality time should be a common practice in the home, regardless of the behavior-shaping that a family may be enduring. Affection and quality time should be constant - it should be the tone of the house.

Affection is best served in **one-on-one time,** quality time spent with just the parent and child. In families with more than one child, try to create opportunities where you can be alone with one child every once in a while. Use that opportunity to be playful, silly, and affectionate.

Without affection and quality time, you're creating a relationship of resentment, distrust, and dislike, where the child won't listen to a ward you have to say.

Affection & Quality Time

Affection
- Loving remarks, appropriate touching, and unique conversations
- Being playful, silly, happy
- Ex.: tickling, games, reading time

Quality time
- One-on-One
- Time spent doing things the child enjoys
- Good time for affection
- Ex.: going out to dinner, reading time, going to the library

Affection and quality time should be constant - it should be the tone of the house.

Parenting Empowerment

Empowering is good, enabling is bad. Basically, empowering a child teaches her to make her own decisions, solve her own problems, and learn how to ask for help. The empowering parent doesn't hover over the child, allows the child to make mistakes, and pushes the child to learn new things.

The enabling parent hovers over the child, and is often overbearing, overprotective, and doesn't allow anyone, especially the school and court system to give the child consequences for behaviors. This teaches the child to learn how to lie, manipulate the system, and that the parent will always fix problems.

There is a way to communicate with your child to empower your child to make his own decisions, called the **Empowering Conversation.**

The Empowering Conversation

1. **Problem Statement**: Kid – "Billy made fun of me today. I started to cry and then everyone made fun of me."

2. **Empathy Statement**: Parent – "Well that stinks. I bet you felt really bad about them laughing."

3. **Behavior Statement**: Kid – "Yeah, I was so mad, that I punched Billy, and now the teacher wants to talk to you."

4. **Empowerment Statement**: Parent – "So what are you going to do about this problem?"

5. **Problem-Ownership Statement**
   Kid – "I don't know, what do I do?"

6. **Advice Statement**: Parent – Explain the options, with possible rewards and consequences

The empathy statement is how the parent verbally expresses impartiality, showing that the child doesn't have to feel guilty, even if he feels mad or sad. This is important to the process in that oftentimes, guilt or shame will lead to anxiety, nervousness, or depression, which can cause a person to shut down and not solve problems.

Once the parent gives help or advice without the child's consent, the parent has taken back the power from the child. **If you offer help or advice, and the child doesn't want it, let it go! DISENGAGE!** If the child does want advice, remind the child that you are not telling the child what to do, and that all you are doing is offering some advice.

In the problem-ownership statement, the child should be able to acknowledge that it is her problem, and she will have to take responsibility and deal with any consequences. Most kids are smart, they know how to work their way through problems. It is the role of the parent to help the child find a healthy plan.

ENABLING

A parent who is enabling is usually overprotective, over-bearing, and constantly hovering over the child with the intention of protecting the child. **Some characteristics of an enabling parent include:**

- Covering for the child, "buying his way out of trouble"
- **Attitude of "I'll do it for you" and "Don't worry about it, I'll take care of it."**
- "Giving in" when the child begins crying, usually buying the toy or candy that the child is screaming for
- **Making excuses for the child, blaming others for the child's situation**
- Making the school change
- Making others unreasonably accommodate the child (through force or manipulation)
- Sometimes a parent will lie to cover for a child

These are some of the more extreme **examples** that we've seen of parents enabling their child:

- We've seen cases where the parent allows the child to stay home from school because he says he's tired. Some cases have had more than 100 absences in a school year.
- Parents claimed that the child didn't do homework, because she had to baby sit while mom was at a friend's house.
- Enabling parents will do homework for the child, giving answers and solutions
- We've seen parents claim that the school system is at fault when the child receives bad grades.
- We've seen false accusations of discrimination, assault, and physical and sexual harassment.

When the parent enables the child, the child learns:
- She can manipulate a situation to get what she wants
- He can lie to get what he wants
- That others control situations when she gets into trouble, and that she can't do anything to fix the problem
- Mom or dad will keep him out of trouble, no matter what he does
- People "owe" her something, even if for no reason, and they should accommodate her with whatever she asks

Some examples of a child manipulating a situation to get what he wants include:
- Having a tantrum in a store to get candy or a toy
- Acting sick to stay home from school
- Playing one parent against the other
- Making excuses for not doing school work

EMPOWERING

A parent who empowers the child is the exact opposite of the enabling parent – consistent when enforcing rules, allows space so the child can experience new things, and engages the child in healthy discussion about a problem that the child is having, . **Some characteristics of an empowering parent include:**

- **Does not always step in when a child has a problem**, teaches the child to ask for help, will only intervene when the child asks for help
- **Encourages: "You can do it" and "I need you to problem-solve."**
- Doesn't "give in" when the child tantrums or argues, uses the "poker face"
- Helps the child problem-solve, instead of making excuses for the child
- Discourages blaming others, making excuses, manipulating, and lying
- Does not overreact when the child falls, cries, or gets hurt
- Helps the child find ways to accommodate the situation, to find solutions
- Always teaching the child that honesty is a great value

These are some **examples** that we've seen of parents empowering their child:

- We've seen cases where the child has broken the law, is taken to the juvenile detention center, and eventually ordered to appear at court, and the parent will make sure that the child accomplishes the requirements that consequences entail. The parent is sympathetic, but also teaches the child that he has to deal with his own consequences.
- During homework sessions, the parent will not do the homework for the child, and will maintain a poker face when the child is learning new skills. Some kids learn to read the parents face, and will guess at the homework answers, until the parent's facial expression tells her that she is correct.

When the parent empowers the child, the child learns:
- She can solve her own problems
- He can make his own decisions
- She learns how to problem-solve, how to get people to help her, and important social skills to be able to communicate and build relationships
- The child learns 'delayed gratification,' meaning that she can do the good behavior when the reward will come later or the reward may never come at all
- Most importantly: the child learns to control his impulses, learns that rewards will come for doing good things, and that his behavior affects his own situation more than any other factors

Some small examples of how empowering a child will affect the child:
- Learning to dress himself and get ready for school in the morning
- The child learns to meet her own needs and will ask for help when she needs it
- Able to pay attention in school and exhibit appropriate behaviors
- Reading and math success depend on parent participation and empowerment

Discipline

Discipline can be a touchy subject, because there are a lot of opinions out there, a lot of media chatter, and many people tend to use their own histories to justify current parenting techniques when it comes to the matter.

The bottom line is this: it's easier to get a child to WANT to follow you by using strategic praise, than it is through disciplinary tactics. Having said that, there are times when a parent must use disciplinary tactics in order to address problems that may be occurring. However, most parents use ineffective techniques, discipline at the wrong time, or fail to follow through with disciplinary action.

The following table includes ineffective disciplinary techniques:

Technique	Why the technique is ineffective
Lecturing	**You have a maximum of 2 minutes to keep your child's attention**, and that is only if the conversation is interactive. You have as long as a kids' cereal commercial to get your message across, even if you have cartoon characters helping you.
Yelling	**Completely breaks down the conversation**, as the child is more concerned with the fear that something bad is happening.
Time Out	Most parents use Time Out for extensive periods of time, usually longer than expected, and then the child gets bored and begins testing the parent. Time Out should only be used to deescalate the situation – **see Chapter 2 on Disengaging.**
Ultimatums	You can't feasibly follow through with every ultimatum. Also, ultimatums are aggressive in nature, and the child will pick up that aggression, and will probably use it at school.
Removing tokens	Too much maintenance – parenting should be easier than that. Tokens can also be a problem for rewarding a behavior, because they are not always available, and there has to be bigger rewards tied to the tokens.
Spanking	**Completely breaks down the conversation**, as the child is more concerned with the fear that something bad is happening. **Physical punishment also breaks down the relationship.**

Your role as a parent is to get your child to do what you need him to do to grow, be happy, and contribute to the family. There are basically two ways to get your children to do what you want them to do: there's the easy way, and there's the hard way.

The easy way is through punishment, bickering, arguing, yelling, lecturing, or using any of the other negative communication skills. Punishment breaks down relationships and the communication process, causing the child to experience emotions related to fear, sadness, and anger, as they try to determine the reason why the parent is acting aggressively. The worst type of punishment is physical, and should never be used in the home! Discipline should only include loss of privileges or retraining the child to do the good behaviors. A lot of parents don't use privileges strategically, allowing the child to take things for granted that should be privileges.

Value Options

Step #1: Assess the situation
- Check your 3 P's
- What are your needs?
- What need is the child trying to meet?

Step #2: Set the scene
During a severe problem-behavior situation, the parent has to use the following skills in order to effectively use Value Options.
- De-escalate the situation:
    1. Use The Calm Tone
    2. Check your Non-Verbal communication
    3. Check your attitude
    4. Disengage
- Strategic Praise
- Parenting Empowerment
- Empathy
- Affection

Step #3: Offer 2 options
- **Option 1: the wanted behavior and the reward**
- **Option 2: the unwanted behavior WITHOUT the reward**
- Make sure the options are things that you can follow-through with – be realistic
- Teach your child about rewards and consequences for decisions

Step #4: Follow-through with the child's decision
- You have to follow through with the decision, you can't turn back
- State the consequences as you follow through
- Allow the child to change his mind
- Use *The Calm Tone*

Use Strategic Praise after your follow-through, praising the child for making a good decision, and for using a Calm Tone. "That was a great decision! I'm so glad that you figured out how to do that, and you did it on your own! And we didn't have to argue or get loud about it – we solved it using a Calm Tone. Thank you so much."

Other important skills for parents

The 3 R's
1. Respite
    - Find healthy ways to get away from your child (babysitter, spouse, grandparents)
    - Use resources in the community
    - Get your child involved in sports, after-school activities; use the local recreation centers, church, or anything else your child is interested in

- Have resources available to maintain your own health and stress levels
  - You're not just a mom or a dad
  - Have your own interests and friends
2. Recreation
   - Have fun as a family
   - Relieve stress as a family
   - Take trips
   - Do things that everyone is interested in
3. Relationship-building
   - This will prevent a lot of stress
   - Your child will be more willing to follow you anywhere and do anything if the relationship is strong
   - Affection & One-on-one time are very important
   - Eating and working are great ways to build relationships
     - Build work ethic
     - Accomplish things that you've been meaning to do anyway
     - Teach your child new skills - this can be as simple as cleaning the house
     - Make it fun!

Prepare for relapse or regression

Relapse and regression, where the child or parent reverts back to "the old way of doing things," is normal in the change process, so it is pointless to get angry about it. There are some things you can do to make it easier.

1. Maintain your skills – keep honing the skills taught in this book.
2. Have a plan
   - Use The Calm Tone
   - Know who to turn to for help – call your old therapist
   - Use Empathy & Affection – it's not just a problem with your child anymore, the entire family is a support network
3. Work through the relapse plan
   - Are there any safety concerns?
   - Should a doctor be involved?
   - What does the school recommend?

Every parent needs a toolbox

In order to create positive behaviors, parents have to possess certain skills. The Top 3 Parenting Skills are:

- **The Calm Tone (Chapter 3)**
- **Effective Reinforcement (Chapter 4)**
- **Parenting Empowerment (Chapter 5)**

Those three skills are critical to creating a functional home life.

The Calm Tone is the ability to use a calm tone in communication, no matter how high the stress level, and regardless of what the child's behavior is. All other communication skills start with a calm tone.

Effective Reinforcement is the ability to see opportunities to reinforce good behaviors and exploit those opportunities to ensure that the child will continue those behaviors. Parents can reduce unwanted behaviors by increasing reinforcement for good behaviors, and reduce stress and the need for punishment.

Strategic praise is a very effective reinforcement technique that doubles as a relationship building technique, and is very low-maintenance compared to other types of reinforcement (rewards, stickers, points, money).

Parenting Empowerment is a parenting skill that teaches independence, problem-solving, and coping skills, preparing the child from an early age to make his own decisions and manage his own consequences. Empowerment is a crucial skill for preventing delinquency, improving school performance, developing healthy relationships, and ensuring job security in the future.

Most parents are great parents, able to read their children, determine their needs, and provide for them quickly, and often with the grace of a well-choreographed ballet or sports team. With the pick-ups, drop-offs, play dates, meal planning, school work, after-school activities, worrying about safety and health – just meeting those needs can be daunting, **and our hats are off to any parent who makes it that far every day.**

> **This book is designed to change parenting skills; it is not an attempt at psychotherapy or "talk therapy" that most people are used to hearing about on daytime television and talk radio.**

Most parents who do satisfy those needs already have skills in their parenting toolbox to make those tasks easier, like sharing the pick-ups and drop-offs with the parent of another child, coordinating play dates both in and out of the home, find quick and nutritious meals with less cleanup, creating habits for healthy hygiene and completing school work, and systems that ensure safety and health, such as code words and schedules.

So, good job! Most of your child's needs as a healthy human being are already being met. This work book is designed to help create habits and systems that will help meet other important needs that affect self esteem and the need for belonging. We have designed a specific skill set that most people already understand, but that we tend to forget about in our fast-paced daily lives.

This book will not discuss medication, because medical intervention should be discussed with your family physician. This book is designed to change parenting skills; it is not an attempt at psychotherapy or "talk therapy" that most people are used to hearing about on daytime television and talk radio.

The traditional "talk therapy" that most adults are accustomed to deals with expressing feelings about their own childhoods or exposing muted and almost hidden emotions about the past. This book presents very little theory designed to change a person's attitude, thoughts, and emotions toward certain subjects that most therapists are accustomed to presenting. Everyone has underlying issues that they are trying to deal with, whether it is painful childhood memories, a disability, or inadequate social or cognitive skills.

However, parenting skills can be developed, and must be developed, to improve the functioning of the home life. Moreover, parents have to set aside those underlying issues and improve the functioning of the home life before they can even attempt to resolve those underlying issues. **This book is designed to offer specific skills that parents can use in their daily lives to implement immediate and profound changes.**

This book contains the treatment model that our practice uses for family therapy. It is a behavior-based model that contains many similarities to the Parent Management Training (PMT) clinical model, a model of mental health therapy that focuses on changing the parent's behavior first, and the child's behavior second, teaching skills that parents can use to effectively reward good behavior, methods to correct wrong behavior, and useful discipline techniques.

PMT has origins in the behaviorism movement earlier in the 20th Century, where most of the work done by B.F. Skinner on operant conditioning and situational influences found uses in everyday life and business in America. Recently, the focus on effective treatment to reduce delinquency and recidivism has compelled treatment practices to implement behavior modification strategies in treatment and prevention programs. Why isn't PMT used more in schools and homes?

> **The bottom line is that all parents want to know ways that will make them better parents.**

First, America loves to hear about other people's problems – look at daytime television. "Talk therapy" has emerged as a popular treatment practice. Most therapists in America are educated and trained in psychotherapy, which is an engaged discussion about the patient's emotions, personal and family history, and attitude. **While psychotherapy is effective in treating a lot of psychological disorders, it probably won't help a parent get a teenager out of bed in the morning.**

Second, some therapists think that telling parents to change is the same as telling them that they are bad parents, and that is certainly not the case. Parents are humans, subject to the stress of everyday life. But all parents want ways that will make them better parents.

To most people, including therapists, therapy means that you go in and talk about your feelings or pent up emotions about the stressors of everyday life. We believe therapy can also teach parents to change behaviors, which can change the stressors of everyday life. **We train parents to change the child's behaviors, ultimately changing the life of the family.** This book emphasizes the most important tools in the PMT model.

Because PMT is a technical clinical model, most of the literature on PMT contains technical language that most people have a hard time understanding. We will use more common language throughout this book.

- We use the term "child" to mean both children and adolescents, ages 0-18.
- We will use the term adolescent when talking about children, ages 12-18.
- Other language will be explained throughout the book.

Changing your behavior as a parent will have many effects:

- Develop a team atmosphere, where your child willingly does things for himself
- Children will become self-managing, meaning less work for the parent
- Less chaos and stress in the home
- More fun
- Fosters a learning environment
- Stronger relationships
- Better performance outside the home: school, work, friends, relationships
- Impacts on the child's future are immeasurable

The Value Set

Topics in this chapter

Behaviors are passed down through generations

Starting with a good foundation
The family system

The family assessment of strengths & needs

Boundaries: knowing when to jump right out!

The Value Set

- **Believe it or not, we are like our parents!**
- Changing your child's behavior requires that **you change your parenting style and role model good behaviors**
- What you say to your kids becomes part of their own self-talk
- There are many parenting skills - but the three core skills handle 90% of the work
- We pass behaviors along to our children, **what behaviors do you want to pass along?**
- Assess your strengths and needs as a parent and as a family
- **Know your value set – the order in which you prioritize your values**
- **Know your family's value set** and protect those values at all costs
- Hone your parenting skills

Behaviors are passed down through generations

Whether we want to admit it or not, most of us end up like our parents, in some weird way, shape, or form. The way we pronounce our R's, how we make a sandwich, our holiday traditions are all passed along through the generations. The same is true for our parenting styles. We may have changed some things about how we show love, communicate, and discipline our children, but some core characteristics rarely change.

> Communication between parents, from parent to child, and from parent to others becomes embedded in the communication style of the child as the child grows and uses the style in his own "self-talk."

These characteristics may be different from one person to the next. Generally, people try to keep the things that they value as good, and discard what they don't value. Others might have inadvertently kept core characteristics that they learned in their childhood, such as communication style. The way that we communicate is a characteristic that is easy to retain, whether we recognize it as healthy or not, and whether we mean to or not. Communication between parents, from parent to child, and from parent to others becomes embedded in the communication style of the child as the child grows and uses the style in his own "self-talk."

Self-talk includes the private speech and thoughts that children develop and ultimately maintain throughout their lives. Self-talk is often used in problem-solving situations, self-comforting situations, and as a coping mechanism. For example, a child may engage in self-talk at school after being teased, thinking to herself, "teasing can't really hurt me, it's just words." The words and ideas in a child's self-talk will usually come from the parent, as the child soaks up information about herself and the world, and eventually creates her own ideology of how the world works.

Self-talk can be critical in how your child shapes his world view. A child who hears obscene language in the home will use obscene language in self-talk and conversations with others. A child who hears positive support for good deeds will use the same supportive language to herself in self-talk. The child will mimic the language and communication patterns that he hears from his parents.

Starting with a good foundation

Universal family principals that support health, happiness, and stability for all family members:

Create a successful mindset: you have to believe that you and your family are worth the energy to that it takes to improve. You have to care, and caring can mean feeling hurt at times, but if you believe it's worth it, and you possess the skills, your lifestyle will change. The parent's happiness is ESSENTIAL to changing a child's behavior and the family's lifestyle, not just a luxury.

Be resourceful and creative: build on positives, strengths, and goals, NOT resentments, weaknesses, and fears. Become the strongest ally for your child's goals. Focus on Win/Win relationship skills. Know who, where, and how to ask for help. Remember the big picture, even though you are goal-focused. Balance the other important areas of life: career, physical health, relationships outside the family, and spiritual and emotional well-being. Be creative and resourceful in fostering those other areas.

> **Be solution-focused, not problem-focused: make a goal, and figure out what needs to happen to attain that goal.**

Be solution-focused, not problem-focused: make a goal, and figure out what needs to happen to attain that goal. Problem: your child gets up from the dinner table and runs around the house spilling food. Goal: Your child remains at the table throughout the meal. What do you need to do to get your child to sit still at the dinner table? Problem: your child is driving you crazy arguing back all the time. Goal: Your child follows instructions, but is also allowed to engage in meaningful conversation at other times. What has to happen to get your child to be a good listener? Problem: Your teenage son consistently comes home after curfew. Goal: Your teenage son comes home sagely at a reasonable time. What do you do to get your teenage son to be home on time?

Successful family changes stem from the quality of family relationships: everything stems from the quality of our relationships with our spouse, children, and other family members. The quality is based on your own investment of time and affection. Start by strengthening or rebuilding positive relationships with your children, increasing strengths and decreasing conflicts, and setting small daily goals.

Break down goals into daily interactions, habit building, and daily structure: choose goals that you want to work on, and then create your strategy to include meaningful interactions with your children every day that focus on those goals. For example: if your child is driving you crazy arguing back all the time, your daily schedule should include small tasks that you and your child could complete together, where you would have prepared praise and a reward for not arguing back, regardless of the completion or quality of the task.

Create your family toolbox: customize, prepare, and organize the parenting skills you need for success within your family. Listed below are some core skills for every parent's toolbox. Which skills are in your toolbox? Which skills do you need to improve?

The family system

The parent is the leader of the family, the captain of the ship. If we expect our children to change, we first have to be able assess and implement change within ourselves and the rules that we have established for the home environment. **Preparing and strengthening yourself as the parent is your primary resource.**

Core parenting skills

CalmTone	Active listening
Affection	Playfulness
Non-verbal communication	Parenting Empowerment
Effective Reinforcement	Accepting feedback
Strategic Praise	Problem-solving
Assertive communication	Decision-making
Parenting leadership	Values maintenance
Role modeling behaviors	Basic life skills
Flexibility	Managing change
Empathetic conversation	Maintaining physical health
Follow through	Developing goals
Disengaging	Relationship building
Healthy diet & exercise	Value options
Healthy outlets	Patience
Respite	Work ethic
Teaching skills	Eliminating negative communication skills
Teaching responsibilities	Financial responsibility

When we talk about resources, we are talking about places, people, or ideas that we can use to help us parent our children. Some resources are internal, meaning they come from within ourselves, such as our communication skills, affection, and the values and goals that we have chosen to live by.

Some resources are external and can be positive or negative influences on our family systems. The family system is a network of relationships that we use as resources in our everyday lives. These relationships aren't always family members, but can include an array of important people.

<u>**Identify the influential roles in your family system:**</u> (circle those that apply)

Parents	Step-parents	Grandparents
School teachers	Church support	Friends
Work relationships	School relationships	Extended family

It is important to be able to recognize the negative or positive influences that these relationships have on your family system. For example, grandparents can be a source of respite, babysitting the kids when you need some time for yourself. However, grandparents can also spoil children with candy and toys, which is not always healthy, even though they are just doing what grandparents do.

It is also important to be able to correct the negatives in a way that preserves relationships, but also maintains the values and goals that you are trying to maintain for your children.

Take a look at those relationships that influence your family, and find similarities within your home. If these relationships are a permanent role, it is in your family's best interest to create positive relationships as a family goal, since those are individuals who will support your shared values for the best interests of your children. Changing these influential relationships can change the progress of your family as a whole in so many ways. The crucial step in effective initial assessment is to change or terminate negative relationships around or within the family system to create positive relationships.

The family assessment of strengths & needs

Let's get started with your family….. Create an effective assessment to map out a successful plan for your family's potential - what is **your family's** story?

Assess your family's overall functioning, strengths, and needs, including significant historic events – starting with your family's present situation – examine your parenting skills, your children's strengths and problems and specific qualities rating your home environment.

<u>Significant family strengths:</u> (circle those that apply)

Emotional	Mental	Physical
Spiritual	Financial	Work ethic

<u>Significant family deficits:</u> (circle those that apply)

Emotional	Mental	Physical
Spiritual	Financial	Work ethic

<u>What Are Your Parenting Skill Strengths?</u> (circle those that apply)

Calm tone	Effective reinforcement	Strategic praise
Assertive communication	Parenting leadership	Role model the skills
Flexibility	Empathetic conversation	Follow through
Disengaging	Teaching skills	Active listening
Accepting feedback	Problem-solving	Use Effective Rationales
Decision-making	Values maintenance	Basic life skills
Managing change	Developing goals	Affection
Relationship building	Value options	Patience
Work ethic	Consistency	Respite
Good Listener	Healthy Affection	Consistent Praise
Healthy Family Relationships	Disagree Appropriately	Positive Asking For Help
Healthy Mealtimes	Healthy Diet	Healthy Exercise
Creative Regular Recreation	Fun Home Activities	Technology Skills
School Success Support	College Focused	Organized Schedule

Clear and Specific Short-Term Goals   Clear and Specific Long-Term Goals

It is important to assess your own strengths and needs, and the strengths and needs of your family in order to develop family goals. Your personal goals are important – you're not just a parent!

Good goals follow the rule of the 3 M's. Remember to make goals that are meaningful, measurable, and malleable, starting with small simple goals.

- Meaningful: must be important to the entire family
- Measurable: you must have a way to evaluate progress
- Malleable: be flexible, change your goals if you have to

Which skills do you need to improve? (circle those that apply)

Calm tone	Effective reinforcement	Strategic praise
Assertive communication	Parenting leadership	Role model the skills
Flexibility	Empathetic conversation	Follow through
Disengaging	Teaching skills	Active listening
Accepting feedback	Problem-solving	Use Effective Rationales
Decision-making	Values maintenance	Basic life skills
Managing change	Developing goals	Affection
Relationship building	Value options	Patience
Work ethic	Consistency	Respite
Good Listener	Healthy Affection	Consistent Praise
Healthy Family Relationships	Disagree Appropriately	Positive Asking For Help
Healthy Mealtimes	Healthy Diet	Healthy Exercise
Creative Regular Recreation	Fun Home Activities	Technology Skills
School Success Support	College Focused	Organized Schedule
Clear and Specific Short-Term Goals		Clear and Specific Long-Term Goals

Chapter 2 - The Value Set

Outline Your Family Ledger: List strengths and needs for your **family.** Include: individual and extended relationships, health, school, work, finances, resources, supports, hobbies, family traits, etc.

Calm tone	Effective reinforcement	Strategic praise
Assertive communication	Parenting leadership	Role model the skills
Flexibility	Empathetic conversation	Follow through
Disengaging	Teaching skills	Active listening
Accepting feedback	Problem-solving	Use Effective Rationales
Decision-making	Values maintenance	Basic life skills
Managing change	Developing goals	Affection
Relationship building	Value options	Patience
Work ethic	Consistency	Respite
Good Listener	Healthy Affection	Consistent Praise
Healthy Family Relationships	Disagree Appropriately	Positive Asking For Help
Healthy Mealtimes	Healthy Diet	Healthy Exercise
Creative Regular Recreation	Fun Home Activities	Technology Skills
School Success Support	College Focused	Organized Schedule

Clear and Specific Short-Term Goals   Clear and Specific Long-Term Goals

Next, identify family history or multi-generational issues and add them to your list of strengths and needs. Discuss and include the unspoken family ledger – unspoken relationship needs and unconscious emotions – and include family secrets and unresolved traumas.

Determining Effective Home Structure Needs For Your Family's Goals

After assessing the family's strengths and needs, the next step will be to set goals to remove your family's negative home structure or lack of home structure. The negative traits should be replaced with positive goals, using a manageable timeline. **You don't want to overload the family change process, but instead use small accomplishments to generate confidence in the process, and trust in each other.**

- Set up home rules that support family goals and values – focus on clear, daily structure with specific and immediate privileges, incentives and consequences.
- Focus on daily, minute to minute, follow through, consistency and role modeling.

- Prioritize main areas of family success: home, school, finances, physical health, strong work ethic, relationships and personal happiness, beginning with the goals and values that are most important.

Boundaries: knowing when to jump right out!

Boundaries are limits that people set and enforce in order to maintain their own goals and values. Most of the time, we try to communicate these boundaries to others with the expectation that they will respect our boundaries.

> **Respecting someone's boundaries means to respect the limits that person has that are meant to protect his values and goals.**

In turn, we try to respect the boundaries of others when they are communicated to us. In some cases, boundaries are understood and actually become cultural norms. For example, while it might be acceptable to "pass gas" in our own homes, we usually refrain when we're in public. Respecting someone's boundaries means to respect the limits that person has that is meant to protect their values and goals.

In order to maintain boundaries, it is important to know our personal values at all times. Within the home environment, the family may have its own set of values that vary from each of the members' values.

You can't reinforce good behavior, unless you know exactly what "good" is. Values are the things that we believe are "good," things we hold dear, things that we want to protect. The value set is a list of values, in order of importance that we refer to when we make goals and actually set out to accomplish those goals.

The value set can be made up of anything, such as people (mom, dad, kids, employees), objects (house, car, money), or ideas (such as honesty, financial strength, or independence). Values can be healthy or unhealthy, some people value smoking, drugs, alcohol, and gambling.

The order of importance of values within the value set is always changing. For example, education and career may be higher in the value set than family in our late teens and early 20's, but family may be prioritized higher once we actually get married and have children. Most people make informal assessments to monitor how their values change, some people write down their values every few months.

The most important thing to know about your value set is the order in which your values are prioritized. This is important in making goals, because sometimes we have to refer back to

> **The value set is a list of values, in order of importance that we refer to when we make goals and actually set out to accomplish those goals.**

the value set to determine which values to enforce over others. Because we have to choose our battles, especially in parenting, we may often have to ignore a lower value in order to reinforce a higher one.

Practice the skill

What is your value set? **List 25 values – in no particular order** – that are important to you – only you. **When you are done brainstorming, go back and put them in order** by writing down the rank number next to that value.

Notice how you will probably change your answers just within the time that you complete this exercise. That is perfectly normal – most people can't pinpoint their values without some deep thought.

Your personal value set:

Rank	Value name	Rank	Value name	Rank	Value name
___	_____	___	_____	___	_____
___	_____	___	_____	___	_____
___	_____	___	_____	___	_____
___	_____	___	_____	___	_____
___	_____	___	_____	___	_____
___	_____	___	_____	___	_____
___	_____	___	_____	___	_____
___	_____	___	_____	___	_____
___	_____				

You can use this space to rewrite your value set in order:

Rank	Value name	Rank	Value name	Rank	Value name
1	_____	10	_____	18	_____
2	_____	11	_____	19	_____
3	_____	12	_____	20	_____
4	_____	13	_____	21	_____
5	_____	14	_____	22	_____
6	_____	15	_____	23	_____
7	_____	16	_____	24	_____
8	_____	17	_____	25	_____
9	_____				

What is your family's value set? List 25 values – in no particular order – that are important to your family, you may want to include input from all family members.

Your family value set:

Rank	Value name	Rank	Value name	Rank	Value name
___	_____	___	_____	___	_____
___	_____	___	_____	___	_____
___	_____	___	_____	___	_____
___	_____	___	_____	___	_____
___	_____	___	_____	___	_____
___	_____	___	_____	___	_____
___	_____	___	_____	___	_____
___	_____	___	_____	___	_____
___	_____				

You can use this space to rewrite your family value set in order:

Rank	Value name	Rank	Value name	Rank	Value name
1	_____	10	_____	18	_____
2	_____	11	_____	19	_____
3	_____	12	_____	20	_____
4	_____	13	_____	21	_____
5	_____	14	_____	22	_____
6	_____	15	_____	23	_____
7	_____	16	_____	24	_____
8	_____	17	_____	25	_____
9	_____				

The Calm Tone

Topics in this chapter

Everything starts with The Calm Tone

Be able to accept feedback

The two faces of parenting

PARENTS: PLEASE DISENGAGE!

The 4 Styles of Communication

Accepting "NO" for an answer

Negative communication habits

The Calm Tone

- **The Calm Tone is the most important skill in the Parenting Toolbox**

- Be able to accept feedback

- The two faces of parenting: The Happy Face & The Poker Face

- The Four Styles of Communication are:
  - Passive
  - Aggressive
  - Passive-Aggressive
  - Assertive

- **Disengage & Ignore** – don't react to unwanted behaviors, and wait for the wanted behavior with a prepared reward or praise

- **Learn how to take "NO" for an answer, and then teach that to your child**

- **Eliminating negative communication skills** is one step toward healthy communication and stronger relationships

Everything starts with The Calm Tone

The most important skill in parenting is The Calm Tone. The Calm Tone is exactly what it sounds like, a calm, non-emotional tone of voice. A lot of times, a stressful situation can cause the tone of one's voice to change in pitch and volume, getting louder and deeper to resonate in one's thoughts, feelings, or demands.

The tone of voice can escalate or deescalate a situation, without the speaker even realizing. To escalate a situation means to increase the intensity and potential risk of the situation, and there are different levels of escalation in any conflict:

Levels of conflict (starting with the least risk)
1. Debate
2. Verbal argument
3. Passive-aggressive threat
4. Yelling
5. Physical force
6. Severe physical force

Obviously the least threatening level of conflict is the debate, where two people express opinions, respect each others' views, and even encourage each other to continue. Severe physical force is obviously the highest risk level, and we oppose any use of force in parenting, including spanking.

We have seen occasions where the child can use physical force against the parent – hitting, kicking, and biting – and we encourage those parents to seek a licensed, professional therapist.

To deescalate a situation means to decrease the level of conflict. We teach the families that we work with that The Calm Tone is the best way to decrease the conflict, and that no matter how high the child is trying to increase the level of conflict, the parent should always show Calm Tone. In fact, the parent should become even calmer as the child escalates.

Reasons for this are evident. First, kids mimic the parent's behaviors. If the parent escalates conflict at home, the child will most likely escalate conflict at home, school, and anywhere else he may have conflict with other people. We are trying to raise healthy, successful, productive kids, and conflict will often counter those goals.

Also, kids are amazingly resourceful and adaptive, and will attempt as many skills as they know in order to meet their own needs. A child will push buttons and boundaries with the hopes of getting what she wants, and if escalating the conflict will help meet the need, she will repeat the behavior every time she needs something.

Third, communication is the basis of learning, asserting wants, needs, and values, and relationship development. The absence of The Calm Tone from the parent's skill set will lead to dysfunctional learning, asserting, and relationships. The child will also learn to communicate without The Calm Tone, and have the same dysfunction throughout his life.

The proof is that some parents intentionally escalate a conflict, because that's what they learned from their parents. But if you truly want a less-stressful, happier home environment, your focus on every situation with your child should be to deescalate.

In the heat of the moment, it may be difficult to deescalate, which is why The Calm Tone is a skill to be mastered. The parent has to be able to realize that a conflict is occurring, recognize the triggers that would usually cause her to argue with the child or yell, and make a conscious effort to remain calm. **The Calm Tone is not a passive-aggressive attempt to**

The Calm Tone

- Use a quiet, normal tone of voice, whether the child is calm and playing or tantrumming and screaming.
- Check your non-verbal style, especially your posture, gestures, and facial expressions, to determine if they are affecting your ability to teach your child important skills.
- If you're not sure if you may be having problems with your other non-verbals, remember this simple rule: continue doing what you were doing before the behavior, act as if the behavior didn't affect you at all.
- The 2 Faces of Parenting:
  - Use the HAPPY FACE when reinforcing a good behavior
  - Use the POKER FACE when you see an unwanted behavior
- Wait for a break in the behavior, prepare a statement of praise, and then reinforce the break:
  "I'm so glad you're going to stop yelling, whenever you feel like talking about what's going on, just let me know."
  "I'm so glad you're not whining anymore, because I can't understand what you want when you're whining. We can talk now, if you want."
- **During a problem-behavior situation, teach The Calm Tone skill first.** Teaching communication skills is critical for the other skills to work! When a child is doing a problem behavior that is preventing communication – yelling, crying, acting aggressively, whining, running around, ignoring – don't worry about anything else at the moment.

control a situation, but merely the tone of voice and non-verbal expressions used in all communications.

"Practicing Calm" should not be used in a punitive manner as with some forms of Time Out. It is respectful as demonstrated by the parent's participation in the quiet calm for the duration needed. The duration is set by the parent, according to the child's ability, the longer they take to achieve calm, the longer the exercise. The duration should correlate to the child's need, as well as teach him direct, immediate reinforcement of the target behavior. The minimum time should meet the level of chaos in the child's mood and body, as well as their successful challenge rate. This rate would challenge their ability to remain calm, while not pushing to the point of their giving up and aggressing further.

The exercise has to have a successful outcome to be effective and, therefore, has to be tailored to the child's abilities for successfully calming. If this exercise is needed, it should probably also be combined with teaching "Not Interrupting" and "Detail Focused Skills." These skills are more effective in combination as the child learns to increasingly control their mood and body to meet appropriate circumstances.

Practicing "Being Calm"

As the level of conflict increases, the parent should become calmer and calmer. You can also practice being calm with your child.

1. Find a quiet place
2. Control possible distractions (move toys out of sight, separate siblings, turn off TV)
3. Affection is an effective non-verbal – hold your child affectionately to start the exercise.
4. Set the tone: "I want us to sit quietly for a few minutes."
5. Use The Calm Tone when the child starts to fiddle and lose interest: "We still have two more minutes, please sit down with me."
6. After a few minutes, use The Calm Tone to start a conversation with the child. Talk about anything – the child's day at school, plans for the weekend, dreams.

The focus of the exercise is on remaining very still and quiet, basically on controlling the body, breath, and mood as it is becoming out of control. Be careful not to overuse or abuse this exercise, only use it when a child clearly cannot sit still and is disrupting a group activity or becoming aggressive and negative attention seeking.

So what does The Calm Tone sound like? Verbally, The Calm Tone is gentle, tranquil, soothing, like the DJ on your local 'Easy Listening' radio station.

"You're listening to the quiet storm on K-A-L-M Radio, your choice for easy listening. I need you to clean your room before you go out and play, and please remember, listeners – Tuesday is laundry day. Please put your sheets and pillow cases in the hamper."

Practice makes perfect – use this exercise regularly until the entire family can effectively sit down and communicate in The Calm Tone, or when trying to address specific instances of aggression or negative attention-seeking behaviors.

The exercise can be used in a preventative or corrective situation. It is more successful in preventative circumstances because the situation is less intense and more easily redirected. It is as simple as asking the child to practice calming down by stating specific directions, to be quiet and to sit very still for a specified time period. The sitting can be altered to fit a standing situation or to not attract attention in public settings.

Eliminating negative communication
- Disengage from the situation
- Prepare a positive statement
- Use a Calm Tone
- State own feelings and thoughts
- Empathize

Be able to accept feedback

The ability to accept feedback means that a parent is able to listen to and be appreciative of feedback in a respectful and calm manner, even if the feedback is coming from the child. Feedback can come in many forms. Someone could be yelling the feedback or merely asserting their own needs.

Most of the time with kids, feedback occurs when the child recognizes that he is having a problem with something, and wants change to occur. Children may not have the vocabulary to fully express their wants, needs, and values, and the parent may have to problem-solve the situation or find some way to draw out the child's feelings.

An example of this can be seen in toddlers, who are usually aware of their needs, but unable to verbalize them. **That can be an example of feedback – the child is telling the parent in her own little way that she wants something, and she wants the parent to provide it.** As children get older, they learn how to verbalize their needs, but are still providing feedback to the parent.

The important thing to understand about accepting feedback as a skill is to remain calm, no matter what the feedback looks like or sounds like. The feedback does not mean that you are a bad parent, and if you are willing to listen to and use the feedback to your advantage, you're actually a great parent.

A lot of times, people can act negatively to feedback, which is not healthy for the communication process, or the relationship. The first step in implementing an open line of communication is eliminating negative communication skills. Sometimes criticism can be very helpful in the change process, and this chapter focuses on how to word, shape and present any feedback, whether it is coming from the parent or the child.

The two faces of parenting

A lot of therapists talk about communication styles and emotions as if they are two separate concepts, but in parenting, the two are so closely linked that one always affects the other. Kids pick up on that. This chapter is designed for parents trying to change a child's behavior. **Although you may use a calm tone of voice in normal, everyday situations, it is also important that you maintain that tone when you're teaching to problem behaviors.**

As parents deal with conflicts and communicate with the child, The Calm Tone uses both verbal and non-verbal communication to express this single emotion: I don't want to argue with you, because I love you, regardless of the outcome of this situation. **The Calm Tone** expresses this to the child: the problem behavior that you're using is not a good way to get what you want.

The Calm Tone also uses non-verbal communication to express the message. Kids can also pick-up on the message sent through the parent's non-verbal posturing, gestures, and facial expressions. A parent may sound calm as she is talking to the child, but may be sending a different signal non-verbally that could confuse the message. There are other non-verbal ways that we express ourselves, such as the clothes that we wear, our physical appearance, proximity, and physical contact, but we'll focus on the three most prevalent.

The two faces of parenting

The happy face is just what it sounds like – happy. Smiling, excitement in the eyes, animated facial expressions – all show the emotion of being happy. People love being happy, and love being around other people who are happy, and the same is true for children. Children are more likely to follow the parent, learn from the parent, and comply with the parent's rules and values, if they are happy with the parent.

The poker face is the other face that parents can use, and has no expression. Poker players watch their opponents, looking for changes in verbals and non-verbals as indicators of thoughts and emotions. In parenting, having no facial expression shows the child that the problem behavior will not affect the outcome of the situation, will not get the child what he wants, and that he should try a different approach to getting what he wants. **You're actually ignoring the unwanted behavior, and waiting for the wanted behavior with a prepared reward or praise.**

> **Healthy Communication Skills**
>
> Focus on positive interaction, not negative communication
>
> Be able to accept feedback
>
> Speak assertively about your own wants, needs and values
>
> Use a Calm Tone
>
> Disengage from conflict
>
> Listen actively
>
> Empower the child through conversation

The parent could even go as far as continuing what she is doing while the child is doing the problem behavior. If you're washing the dishes when the child starts to tantrum, keep washing the dishes. Prepare for a break in the tantrum, and prepare to praise the child for stopping the tantrum. Then teach the wanted behavior.

It is important to keep in mind that childhood is a learning process, so any other facial expression will be counterproductive to the learning process. Anger may cause the child to withdraw from communication, and may worry more about the punishment than learning how to get what he wants. A mad face or showing disappointment may cause the child to be more concerned with fixing the new problem (dad is disappointed) than problem-solving her needs without using the problem behavior.

Once the child stops the problem behavior, it is important for the parent to shift back to

If you don't remember anything else from this chapter, remember this: **ignore the unwanted behavior, and wait for the wanted behavior with a prepared reward or praise. Then praise the heck out of the good behavior.**

the happy face in order to praise or reward the child for stopping the behavior. Shifting between the happy face and poker face is an important part of reinforcing wanted behaviors and avoiding the stresses that come from having to punish or lecture the child.

Don't try to teach anything else at that moment, except that you want the conversation to happen in a calm tone, no matter what problem behavior the child is doing that is a barrier to communicating – yelling, crying, acting aggressively, whining, running around, ignoring – teaching communication skills comes first!

PARENTS: PLEASE DISENGAGE

We don't have to describe a child's tantrum, parents have seen it all – yelling, kicking, throwing things, falling to the floor. And we also know that it can be very difficult to maintain a calm tone during a full blown tantrum. The situation gets tougher as the child gets older and bigger, and when the child becomes an adolescent the childhood tantrum will turn into a screaming match.

Disengaging

1. Let the child know that you're going to disengage.
2. Walk away and find something else to do.
3. When the child is calm, reinforce her calming down.
4. Teach the healthy communication skills. (P.23)
5. Teach other skills only after "Calm Tone" has been resolved

Disengaging is a skill that a parent can use to deescalate a conflict, removing himself from the situation to regroup and return with a calm tone. Disengaging reinforces the calm communication process, showing the child that the parent is not willing to argue, and that arguing and tantrumming is not a good way to assert wants, needs, and values. Disengage means to remove yourself from the situation, and then return after the child is calm.

There is a process for disengaging. First, let the child know that you are disengaging by saying, "I'm going to walk away right now, and I'll come back when you've calmed down. If you can calm down before I come back, come and find me, and then we can talk."

Walk away and find something else to do to show that you are not affected by the conflict. Use the poker face to show that you're not mad or happy about the behavior. When the child is calm, praise her for calming down. You can then teach the skills for healthy communication – being a good listener, accepting feedback, focusing on a positive interaction.

The 4 Styles of Communication

There are four general ways that people communicate:
- Passive
- Aggressive
- Passive-Aggressive
- Assertive

We recommend assertive communication as the primary mode of communication, the healthiest way to state wants, needs, and values, while also maintaining trust and respect from others. In this section, we will describe all four styles of communication, including pro's and con's, motivations, outcomes, and the effects on relationships.

Becoming assertive

It can be very difficult to change the way you communicate – communication is the first skill that we learn. It is reinforced by the family and develops through childhood, and is fortified as we start to learn that we are meeting needs and maintaining values through our communication. What we don't realize is the potential stress and problems that could be avoided by becoming more assertive. However, you can become more assertive.

First, practice in a mirror. Your non-verbal communication is the first thing to change. Use an open, non-threatening posture, go easy on the gestures, and check that your facial expressions aren't sending the wrong messages. Practice the two faces of parenting, as you watch yourself in the mirror. Look happy when you're making positive statements, and use your poker face when you're not happy. Find any non-verbals that may seem threatening, closed, or anxious.

Practice all of your different faces in the mirror, even look at yourself when you're mad. You will probably be very surprised to see just how scary your mad face can be. Kids know what a mad face looks like, even at an early age, and are able to sense their own fear when they see the mad face. Ask a four-year old about a Jack-O-Lantern, and he'll probably tell you the Jack-O-Lantern is mad and scary. It's also amazing that kids that young can sense anger and fear in movies by watching facial expressions of the actors.

Being assertive
1. Practice your non-verbals in a mirror
2. Prepare a few useful, everyday statements, using the assertive style
3. Practice disengaging – at least long enough to think of your next statement
4. Say, "No," when you want to, and be able to accept, "No," from others.
5. It is okay to let other people make their own decisions, it is okay for you to make YOUR OWN decisions.

Second, practice some assertive statements that you can use every day.

"I need you to get dressed and ready for school." ASSERTIVE

"I want you to concentrate on your homework." ASSERTIVE

"I feel happy when you to help me with dinner." ASSERTIVE

Notice how changing the wording of the sentence will change the tone of the message:

"You need to get dressed and ready for school." AGGRESSIVE

"You need to concentrate on your homework." AGGRESSIVE

"You need to help me with dinner." AGGRESSIVE

By practicing a few useful statements, you will probably develop the habit of using *want, need, and feel* in all of your everyday communications.

Third, practice disengaging – start to notice the things that make you engage in arguments, discussions, or problem behavior situations – and focus on not reacting. Instead of engaging, use the time to prepare your assertive statement. You should account for the skill you want to teach at that moment, your own values and goals, and the level of the conflict, if any.

Fourth, it is okay to say, "No." It is okay to set a boundary, if the other person is asking you to do something that you're not willing to do. And, you don't have to apologize for saying, "No." Most people don't realize that the assertive style is the most common style of communication, which means, that most people will understand your, "No," and will respect your boundary.

Also, you should respect the other person's boundaries as well, if they tell you, "No." This maintains mutual respect in the relationship, so that neither person harbors any resentment of feelings of victimization. However, don't say, "No," just because the other person has told you, "No." That would be an example of passive-aggressive communication. If your values support a decision, and you're happy with it, go for it.

That is the essence of assertive communication. If everyone is saying that they are okay with the decision, statements, or feelings in a given situation, then everyone has to be okay

Passive – "Walked all over"

- Avoids conflict at all costs, by allowing others to have their way
- Does not assert own wants and needs
- Agrees to everything every time
- Creates Lose-Win outcomes
- May often feel victimized
- Feels that speaking up will lead to rejection by others
- May not know own needs, assumes the values and goals of others
- Usually indicates lower self esteem
- Learned from parent or abuse
- May feel like the strength of the relationship is more important than the conflict
- Own needs are not met, may not have own needs or values
- May enter relationships with others who will take advantage of passivity
- Always backs down from conflict

Passive-Aggressive – "Hidden Aggression"

- Combines the Passive and Aggressive styles of communication:
- Wants to be aggressive, but usually fears rejection
- Uses inappropriate sarcasm, procrastination, sabotage, and other HIDDEN behaviors in an attempt to meet needs
- Often creates Lose-Lose or Lose-Win outcomes
- Hidden agendas undermine relationships
- May be able to gain the trust of others, but eventually loses trust because of ulterior motives
- May often feel victimized, until acting out through impulse behaviors
- Likely learned behaviors and communication from parents – parent was either passive, aggressive or passive-aggressive

Aggressive – "The Bully"

- Tone and non-verbals may often be threatening to others
- Intentional disregard for others' feelings and needs, no empathy
- Meets own needs by intimidating and controlling others
- Creates Win-Lose outcomes
- Learned in childhood that aggression and violence are the only ways for communicating
- Usually indicates family history of violence
- Usually indicates lower self esteem, stemming from a sense of inadequacy in one or more areas of life
- Relationships are usually less important than power and control, most relationships will fail
- May enter relationships with others who will be submissive

Assertive – "Direct with Respect"

- Asserts wants, needs, values in a direct and open manner
- Uses "I want," "I need," or "I feel" statements
- Ex. "I want our family to communicate better." "We need to clean the house."
- Able to accept rejection, can accept "no" for an answer
- Creates Win-Win outcomes
- Develops relationships based on open communication
- Respects the needs and values of others
- Gains trust and respect from others
- Often meets needs, knows how to ask for help, and problem-solves effectively
- Usually maintains own boundaries, and respects the boundaries of others

The most effective way to communicate!

> **Fight the good fight means to choose the battles that are important enough to fight, and let the other battles go. The battles should be chosen according to your value set.**

with the outcomes. No one person can come back and blame, retract, or make excuses if everyone was okay with the situation in the first place.

Fifth, it is important to let other people – including your kids – make their own decisions, and to even encourage others to make their own decisions. Also, it is okay for you to make YOUR OWN decisions. Sometimes it can be very hard to let go, but it is also important to fight the good fight.

Fight the good fight means to choose the battles that are important enough to fight, and let the other battles go. The battles should be chosen according to your value set. For example, let's say a parent struggles with the child every morning to get dressed for school, and when he does, he never wears what the parent wants. The most important battle at the moment is to get the child ready on time, the choice of attire is secondary. Parents have to learn to let go of secondary problems, and focus on one step at a time.

Start by practicing the smaller skills, such as The Calm Tone; and build up towards using the assertive communication style in every conversation, whether you're at home, work, or school. Assertive communication, like all of these skills, has to be role modeled to children, and will create better long-term opportunities for them.

Body Language

- **Posturing** is the way a person stands in relation to the other person in the conversation. A range of emotions could be expressed in the way a person postures her body. Someone could perceive aggression if the posture is threatening, such as being bent over the other person, or standing in someone's personal space. Standing close to someone could also indicate affection or a feeling of closeness.

- **Gestures** include the motions made with the hands and arms, including non-motion, such as folding the arms across the chest or clutching a door frame. Gestures can present warmth, openness, and nurturing, such as with a hug or open arms. They could also present the opposite, with the arms folded across the chest, or holding the arm out to distance the other person.

- **Facial expressions** are probably the most transparent of the non-verbal styles, and can include the entire range of emotions expressed by blinking eyes, frowning, smiling, or any other facial contortion. It is here that we will discuss the two faces of parenting: the happy face and the poker face.

Accepting "NO" for an answer

Being able to accept "NO" for an answer is a very important skill, and most people don't realize that it's a skill. How do you react when someone tells you "NO"? **This table shows how people using the 4 different styles of communication react to being told "NO."**

Style	Reaction to being told "NO"
Passive	People who are passive are usually okay when they are told "NO," and probably won't pursue the matter any further. Passive people are usually unlikely to assert their own wants, needs, and values, and will go along with what others tell them to do.
Aggressive	Aggressive people may become angry when told "NO," and will likely use force, threats, intimidation, or other control tactics to press the issue. They will usually continue until they find an "out," a way to end the conflict without "losing face."
Pass-Aggr	Passive-Aggressive people will usually use sarcasm, hidden aggression, or make "snide remarks," when told "NO." These people **want** to meet their wants, needs, and values, but are scared to assert themselves, for fear of rejection.
Assertive	The assertive person remains calm and polite, and may even ask, "Is there any way we can make this work for both of us?" This person begins the problem-solving process when told "NO," but is also able to say, "Well, thank you for your time," and then walk away okay.

It is easy to see how the assertive style is the most effective for maintaining healthy boundaries. Being able to accept "NO" for an answer is the same as being able to respect the boundaries that other people create for themselves.

There is a way to practice the skill of accepting "NO" for an answer in an assertive manner:

1. **Assertive statement:** Ask for what you want. Be polite and respectful, but be direct. "I need to borrow the car, because some of my friends are going to the basketball game."
"NO"

2. **Feeling statement:** I feel _____, BECAUSE I _____
_____. I
would like to _____.
"NO"

3. **Thankful statement:** Be appreciative of the things you have. Keep the relationship open for future needs. "Well, thanks anyways, I appreciate you listening, and I respect your decision."

Negative communication habits

Most of the skills in this workbook are proactive steps in CREATING a better home environment. This section will focus on EXTINGUISHING some of the behaviors that we may use as parents, or that we may see in our children. **Some of the negative communication skills that are most common include:**

- Interrupting
- Aggression
- Passivity
- Passive-Aggression
- Wrong message
- Impatience
- Lecturing

We've discussed Passive, Aggressive, and Passive-Aggressive communication; so, we'll focus on the other four negative communication habits.

Interrupting

Interrupting in general is bad for the communication process, breaking down people's desire to want to communicate, and creating feelings of contempt as a person struggles to express opinions, thoughts, ideas, or emotions.

> Interrupting is bad for the communication process, breaking down people's desire to want to communicate.
>
> **Parents who lecture are unable to retain the child's attention long enough to effectively express the message.**

Children usually interrupt conversations when they are seeking attention from the parents. Every parent has probably been in the middle of a conversation – in the store, at home, at the park, on the phone – when their child has suddenly interrupted with, "Mom, mom, mom, mom, mom, mom, mom." If ignored, the trail of moms would continue forever.

That is a perfect time to use The Calm Tone and Disengaging, and then practice Being Calm with the child before teaching Assertive Communication.

Lecturing is usually ineffective

Parents who lecture are unable to retain the child's attention long enough to effectively express the message. Parents who lecture usually drone on and on trying to teach the behavior as if it were skill, like tying shoelaces or parallel parking. Lecture has to be shortened so that ideas have to be expressed within seconds and have to be organized in cause and effect statements, in order for the child to make logical connections between the behavior and the consequence.

There has been a lot of research in the fields of therapy, education, and juvenile justice concerning contact with a child or adolescent. The emergence of "Brief Therapy" has extended into family practices, couples therapy, and even into business trainings. Classrooms have shifted from a lecture-based philosophy to an interactive skills-based team environment. Intelligent treatment design has to account for the attention span of the child, and lecturing just doesn't work.

Wrong message

A person may express calmness and openness through his non-verbals, but may send the wrong message by sending the wrong verbal message. Even a calm tone and demeanor can express anxiety, nervousness, or anger when the message is flawed. The result is usually feelings of contempt when people misinterpret what you said and you feel that you're always correcting problems.

> A person may express all of the calmness and openness in the world through her non-verbals, but may send the wrong message by sending the wrong verbal message.
>
> Impatience will usually cause a person to act impulsively, jump to conclusions, misinterpret messages, or interrupt.

Verbal cues are an important part of the message, and are usually those conveyed through the qualities of the voice, such as tone, volume, rhythm, pitch, pausing and inflection. Changing the tone of any word in the sentence can change the message that is being sent.

For example, say the following sentences to yourself, emphasizing the word in italics:

I didn't steal the cookie. (Infers that someone else stole the cookie)

I *didn't* steal the cookie. (Infers that I didn't steal the cookie)

I didn't *steal* the cookie. (Infers that I had permission to eat the cookie)

I didn't steal the *cookie*. (Infers that I stole something, but not the cookie)

An easy way to manage the message is by constantly checking your value set. By knowing your values, it will be easier to maintain boundaries and frame your assertive statements to send the message that you want to send.

Impatience

Impatience will usually cause a person to act impulsively, jump to conclusions, misinterpret messages, or interrupt. Being able to listen patiently allows others to feel like they are respectfully able to express emotions, thoughts, and opinions, and that those expressions are respected by the listener. This maintains the lines of communication, and ultimately the relationship.

Being able to patiently listen to someone also creates a feeling that the person can communicate without being judged. This is an important part of feeling respected, and is especially important to adolescents.

Chapter 3 - The Calm Tone

Effective Reinforcement

Topics in this chapter

Reward me with your undying love... or candy

What is reinforcement?

What is *Effective* Reinforcement?

Strategic Praise – the most effective reward

Maslow's Hierarchy of Needs

Negative to positive

Rewards come in different shapes

The effects of affection

Effective Reinforcement

- Thanks for reading this chapter! (There's an example of reinforcement)
- Positive reinforcement is the most effective way to shape a child's behaviors
- Tactical Parenting – parenting with a plan
- Separate Life's Lessons – teach one lesson at a time

Strategic Praise

- Change your own reactions to the bad behavior from 'negative' to 'no reaction': DISENGAGE!
- Target specific good behaviors to increase
- Immediately reward the first time you see the target behavior
- Over-emphasize the praise the first few times you see the good behavior
- Avoid lecturing when praising, keep the praise directed at the good behavior.
- As the old behavior disappears, use generalized statements of the long-term life values when praising the new behaviors

Reward me with your undying love… or candy

The first thing we need to talk about is why behaviors exist. People do things to meet their needs, and will keep doing those things as long as they get what they want.

Humans find a means for meeting their needs. Most people meet needs in healthy ways, and some people meet their needs in unhealthy ways. Children are especially keen to finding ways to meet their needs, but their perceptions of what they need are often muddled with what they *want*. Children are also less likely to look at long-term needs, wants, and values, so they go after what they want immediately. Behaviors can escalate quickly from tapping the parent to tugging on the parent, from nagging to whining, and eventually to a full tantrum.

> **People do things to meet their needs, and will keep doing those things as long as they get what they want.**

The purpose of this chapter is to develop parenting skills that can teach children to meet their needs in healthy ways that can eventually empower them and reduce the stresses of everyday life. **Reinforcement is the most effective way to shape a child's behaviors.**

What is reinforcement?

Before we discuss how parents can shape a child's behaviors, we should explain certain words to lay a ground work for reinforcement:

1. Reinforcement means strengthening support. In parenting, reinforcement means supporting a behavior by reacting positively to the behavior. There are two different types of reinforcement, which we'll describe later, but for now we are only going to refer to the act of supporting a behavior as "reinforcement."

2. A reward is something that is given when the child does something good, and can also be called a reinforcer. There are many different examples of rewards:

Types of rewards	Examples	
Food & Snacks	• Healthy snacks • Candy • Gum	• A meal that the child wants • Eating at a place the child wants to eat
Tokens	• Point system • Stickers & stars	• Toys • Concert tickets • Other items bought for the child that represent abstract rewards, like satisfaction of doing a good job, good grades, etc.
Privileges	• TV • Computer • Video games	• Going to a friend's house • Going for a ride • Whatever the child wants to do in free time
Social reinforcers	• Strategic praise • Attention • Appropriate physical contact	• Affection • Conversation
Removal	• Taking away something unwanted • Stopping a bully	• Needing to leave the classroom • Easing pain • Easing worry or anxiety • Not having to finish vegetables

Obviously kids have to go out and play, need affection, and they have to eat, even if there is nothing to reward. We're not saying that these things can only be used as rewards. We are saying that parents could use these things as rewards whenever possible.

3. A stimulus could be anything in any situation that causes someone to act. Anything can be a stimulus – we could even break down situations into smaller stimuli, down to every word and non-verbal in a conversation. **In parenting situations, we're more concerned about the child's general behavior in a situation and how the parent reacts to that behavior.**

4. Attitude is basically someone's outlook on a situation, how a person thinks and feels in a situation, and how the person's body reacts.

   a. **Thoughts** – the actual thoughts in a person's mind, during the situation, both conscious and sub-conscious. Thoughts can be any cognitive process in reaction to a stimulus.

b. **Physical reaction** is how the body naturally reacts to a stimulus. It is important to be aware of this reaction, because it could be seen as a non-verbal signal to the other person. Some examples of how the physical body can act in a situation are:

- Heart beat quickens
- Breathing quickens or slows
- Muscles tense
- Smiling

- Chest could puff up
- Blinking
- Twitching
- Crying

c. **Emotions** – feelings that are caused by the stimulus. The four basic human emotions are mad, sad, glad, and scared. All other emotions are more or less intense versions of those four emotions, or combinations of those emotions. Some examples include:

Mad	Sad	Glad	Scared
Disturbed	Unhappy	Amused	Apprehensive
Negativity	Depressed	Comforted	Nervous
Bitter	Grief	Awe	Repentant
Angry	Remorse	Confident	Terror
Disgusted	Loss	Cool	Phobic
Hate	Despair	Elated	Paranoid
Rage	Indifferent	Loved	Vulnerable

5. The behavior is what this whole workbook is about: how do we become the most effective parents, so that our child's behaviors are exactly what we want them to be? Anytime we refer to "behavior" in this workbook, we are talking about the child's behavior in any given situation.

6. Reaction to the behavior is what we are calling **the parent's reaction to the child's behavior.** The intention of this workbook is to make parents look at how they are reacting to the child's behaviors that reinforce those behaviors. **The parent can choose not to react,** which would still be a reaction.

How are behaviors formed?

The stimulus or situation affects the child's attitude in that brief moment in time. The situation can change the attitude – bad or good – or the attitude can stay the same. The attitude – thoughts, emotions, and physical reaction – then affect the behavior, which in turn causes the parent to react.

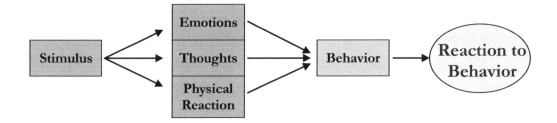

This is the Behavior Shaping Model: The arrows in the figure represent the causal chain – in other words, what affects what.

Those three things then affect how we behave in reaction to the situation, which will result in some outcome, which could range from an extremely negative consequence to an extreme reward. **Emotions, thoughts, and the way our bodies physically react in a situation make up our attitude in any given situation.**

When we get a negative consequence, we are less likely to behave the same way the next time the same type of situation occurs. We may have the same emotions and physical reactions that next time, but our thoughts will change as we remember the previous attempt that produced the negative outcome, and **we weigh the probability of receiving the same negative outcome against changing the behavior to produce a better outcome.**

Usually, a negative consequence will cause a person to change the behavior the next time he is in that same situation.

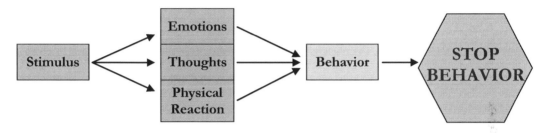

To change the behavior, we have to be able to recognize the situation and stop ourselves before we act. This is where our problem-solving skills and ability to ask for help will help us shape a new behavior that will produce a positive outcome.

When we receive a positive outcome during a situation, we are more likely to use that successful behavior every time we are in the same situation. Over time, we will continue to reproduce that behavior, each time our thoughts include the memory of previous successful outcomes.

That is how habits form, by consistently reproducing behaviors that experience and time have proven will get you what you want. Every time we recognize a situation that we have been in before, we'll remember our experience and reproduce the effective behavior.

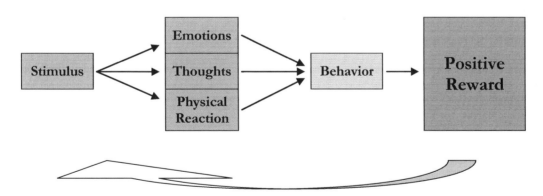

The parent's role in this cycle

The parent's job in the behavior-shaping cycle is to wait for the child to do the wanted behaviors, and then reward the heck out of them. That requires a plan, a prepared reward, and patience to wait for the behavior to happen. That seems like a lot of work, but it will ultimately pay off by empowering the child to project the outcomes in the behavior. **The**

> The parent's job in the behavior-shaping cycle is to wait for the child to do the wanted behaviors, and then reward, reward, reward!
>
> That requires a plan, a prepared reward, and patience to wait for the behavior to happen.

rewards will inevitably decrease as habits form over time, meaning that you'll have to do less parenting once the behavior is habit.

For kids who develop an internal locus of control, parents can also try to work on realizing the emotions, thoughts, and physical reactions. Children who can shape their emotions, thoughts, and physical reactions to fit the desired outcome, then the behavior is arbitrary, because it will probably fit the outcome needs as well.

That is tough to do, but will create the best opportunities for the child in the long run. Refer to Chapter 5 to see the effects of an internal locus of control on school achievement, wanted behaviors, and potential job performance.

What is *Effective* Reinforcement?

There are two types of reinforcement: positive and negative. **Both positive and negative reinforcement will increase the likelihood that the person will continue that specific behavior.**

The difference between the two is that positive reinforcement means that something was gained after the behavior, and negative reinforcement means that something was taken away after the behavior eliminating something that the person thought was negative or hurtful.

Positive reinforcement	Negative reinforcement
Rewarding the person after the behavior— attention, candy, praise – will make her continue doing that behavior	Taking away something after the behavior that will make her continue doing that behavior to alleviate the pain.
Both types of reinforcement are "rewards," one giving something of value, and the other is taking away something that is not wanted.	

For example, children naturally seek attention, and will find ways to get it. Let's say that Alex is bored, and is looking for attention from his brother, and repeats the brother's name. "Jimmy, Jimmy, Jimmy, Jimmy, Jimmy, Jimmy, Jimmy." Jimmy then screams, "Stop saying my name!" Alex's behavior was to repeat his brother's name, and Jimmy responded by screaming. Alex got what he wanted from the behavior, which was Jimmy's attention, meaning that Jimmy's scream was positive reinforcement for Alex's behavior, and Alex will continue to annoy Jimmy.

Negative reinforcement can be found in the same example, but for Jimmy. Jimmy's behavior was to scream at Alex in an attempt to quiet him, because Jimmy thought Alex's behavior was annoying. Alex stopped his behavior, giving Jimmy negative reinforcement. Jimmy will remember the next time Jimmy is being annoying, and repeat the behavior of screaming at Alex. **Effective reinforcement is a tactical parenting technique that requires the parent to plan out the behaviors that are wanted and a reward that will reinforce that behavior.** It requires that you make a plan to change a behavior, prepare yourself to reward or praise that behavior, and then be patient enough to wait for the behavior to occur. You also have to be patient when you see the unwanted behaviors.

The 3 P's of Effective Reinforcement

1. Plan: develop a plan based on the behaviors that you want your child to do more often

    a. Based on your value set – determine what values you want to work on with your child

- Be specific – what exactly are you trying to change?
- Fight the good fight – change the important things first
- If you feel overwhelmed with the changes that you want to make, focus on the most important ones first
- Calm Tone should be first – to eliminate the stresses of arguments, whining, begging, and crying
- Empowerment is important for the child's growth

    b. Be realistic

- Consider your child's age, level of understanding, cognitive abilities, vocabulary limitations
- Set small goals first to build confidence
- Make goals achievable and help your child succeed, failure will stop the change process

    c. Write things down, keep things simple

2. Prepare: prepare your reward and how you are going to present it

    a. Rewards don't have to be tangible, Strategic Praise is the best reward in any situation

    b. Be specific

- What can you use to reward the child?
- What will the child value?
- How will you communicate that to the child?
- Be realistic – don't promise anything you can't give

    c. Commit the entire family

- Make sure your significant other is on board
- Teach older siblings to help you reinforce wanted behaviors in younger children
- Communicate your goals to your family
- Take precautions not to reward the wrong behaviors

3. Patience

- Be patient, wait for the behavior, wait for the change
- When you see the behavior: reward, reward, reward
- If you don't see the behavior: teach, teach, teach
- Use a Calm Tone when teaching, and be assertive with your needs
- Use "I need," "I want," or "I feel" statements
- Practice the wanted behavior with your child
- Connect the behavior to the bigger picture

Practice the 3 P's:

1. Plan

What behaviors do you want to disappear?

1.	6.
2.	7.
3.	8.
4.	9.
5.	10.

What behaviors do you want to see?

1.	6.
2.	7.
3.	8.
4.	9.
5.	10.

Which ones are most important?

1.	3.
2.	4.

2. Prepare

- What can you use to reward the behavior?_____
- Is it suitable?_____ Can you follow through with that reward?_____
- Tell other family members: "Hey, I want to work on _____'s behavior, especially the way he/she _____ _____. I need you to help me teach him how to _____ _____."
- What are you going to say to the child when you see the behavior? "That's so great that you _____. That was important, because _____. Since you did that, I'm going to _____."

3. Patience

- Be patient
- Learn to disengage from the unwanted behaviors, and wait for the wanted behaviors to appear.
- If you see the unwanted behavior, use a Calm Tone to teach the child the behavior that you want to see:

  "I need you to _____ when you want _____. It's important, because _____. Let's practice how to _____."

  "That's great! I knew you would be good at _____, and it'll make it easier for me to _____."

Practicing is a great way to teach the behavior, because it shows the child exactly what you're expecting, and then the child is immediately given strategic praise after showing you that he can do the behavior.

Strategic Praise statements use the same language, except the Praise is said first, and is followed by the teaching:

"That's great that you _____,
I'm so happy that you did that! Since you did that, I'm going to _____
_____."

"I need you to do that more often, okay? It's important, because _____
_____."

The last part of that Strategic Praise statement is where the parent has to connect the behavior to the bigger picture, which will help the child begin to use critical thinking skills to engage in abstract thought. That is important because your child will use most of the behaviors that you will be reinforcing in other settings, like school, work, with friends, and in important relationships.

For example:

- Listening skills are important in all aspects of life.
- Communication skills are important in all aspects of life.
- Concentrating on finishing a household chore will equate to work ethic.
- Helping the family complete household chores will equate to work ethic.
- Asking for help is important to the self esteem.

Strategic Praise – the most effective reward

Praise can be shown to children through so many creative and sincere approaches that fit our personality. Simply put, praise is a communication of admiration for something achieved, or recognition to someone for a job well-done. It is a way of expressing gratitude to that person for a specific behavior, but often communicates the more profound message of just how important they are to us.

Strategic praise is praise with a plan. It is knowing what behaviors you want to increase, and when and how to reinforce them.

Much research has been done on the affects of praise, both in the home with children and at work with employees and co-workers. Most of the research shows that consistent praise of good acts decreases the need for consequences for bad acts.

The Yes/No Game is a great group activity that shows the differences between strategic praise and consequences, having been played countless times at leadership seminars and trainings.

The game begins with the group picking one person to be sent out of the room. The group then decides on a task for that person to complete. In the first round, the group cannot give the person any hints as to what the task is, and will only be able to say the word, "No," when the person is doing something wrong or walking in the wrong direction. The person is brought back into the room, and is timed as he attempts to complete the task. Also, someone in the group records the number of times the group says, "No."

The second round is conducted the same as the first, sending the person out, choosing a task, and then bringing the person back in to complete the task. This time, however, the group can only say, "Yes," when the person is doing something right or walking in the right direction. The person is again timed and the number of 'Yes'" are recorded.

Strategic Praise

- Use a Calm Tone and positive statements
- Timing is everything – try to praise as soon as you see the good behavior
- Short, sweet, and to the point – remember that praise is a reward, and a reward is supposed to be enjoyable

That's great that you _____, I'm so happy that you did that! I need you to do that more often, okay? It's important, because _____.

The last part of that Strategic Praise statement is where the parent has to connect the behavior to the bigger picture. This helps the child begin to use critical thinking skills to engage in abstract thought.

Usually the game has the same results:
- The person completing the task usually feels frustrated more during the 'No' round, than in the 'Yes' round.

    Frustration can hinder problem-solving skills in children, meaning that the frustration from criticism can actually make your child less likely to learn how to successfully solve his own problems. If constant consequences or negative feedback are continually influencing a child's frustration levels, the child could develop long-term problems with lack of motivation, apathy and anger.

    Parents who struggle with negative relationships with their children can use strategic praise as a foundational skill to **change the quality of the relationship before focusing on changing the target behaviors.**

- The group usually has to say 'No' more than 'Yes,' and amazingly often tends to start yelling 'No' during that round as the frustration level builds over time. The energy level also builds in the 'Yes' round, but it often feels more like excitement than frustration.

    To a parent, this means that you're spending A LOT of energy being negative, wasted energy that could be spent doing something else, when you could be spending less energy positively praising your child when he is doing something right.

- The person usually takes longer in the 'No' round, and sometimes doesn't even finish. The negative consequence causes the person to shutdown. This is probably the most important reason to emphasize the importance of praise – **praise will motivate your child to continue to learn and grow, not discourage her from learning.**

The difference between praise and criticism	
Praise:	**Criticism:**
Motivates	Frustrates
Empowers	Discourages
Enables learning	Inhibits learning
Uses less energy	Requires more energy

Maslow's Hierarchy of Needs

Abraham Maslow was among the first in the field of social psychology, the study of individuals' values and behaviors in relation to a larger social setting. Although most of his work did not have scientific foundation, he did develop a theory that is still used in business and social work, known as the "Hierarchy of Needs."

Basically, Maslow determined that most humans have a similar set of needs, which drives behavior. The desire to meet a need motivates an individual to complete tasks and meet needs, so the amount of motivation is directly linked to productivity. Maslow described five main classifications of needs, in order of importance: physiological, safety, love and belonging, self-esteem, and self-actualization. He argued that these needs form a hierarchy, with physiological needs for survival at the base, being the most important needs to fulfill.

Maslow's model doesn't represent all human needs or allow for individualism, but it is a good way to take a simple look at basic human motivations. Each level of need must be met in order to meet the next level of needs. For example, one cannot truly achieve self-actualization, unless all other needs are met at that particular time. Maslow also recognized that a person can regress, moving back down the hierarchy, if he feels that a lower need is threatened or is no longer being met. Motivation changes to meet that need, and the person acts on that behavior until homeostasis is achieved.

Maslow's Hierarchy of Needs

5. **Self-Actualization:** motivates growth as a human being to realize potential for ideal self concept

4. **Esteem:** respect from self & respect from others

3. **Belonging:** the need to feel loved and accepted within family and peer groups, develops a sense of community and bond with others

2. **Safety:** motivates a person to find a safe, stable, supporting environment, free from abuse or neglect

1. **Physiological:** air, water, food, activity, sleep, and sex – survival needs

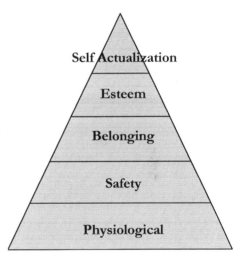

Most people will find healthy ways to meet these needs, finding jobs to be able to pay for food and shelter, belonging to supportive social groups, such as families, marriage, and school and work environments. Most people also learn healthy behaviors to meet these needs, such as healthy social skills and humor as a way of connecting with people, and honesty and openness to earn respect.

Some people find unhealthy ways to meet these needs, such as stealing food and water to support survival and manipulating people to establish a safe and accepting environment. Some people join unhealthy groups, such as gangs, unhealthy peer groups or marriages, in order to meet the need for belonging and acceptance. The reason is that humans are susceptible to feelings of inadequacy, nervousness, anxiety, and depression when needs are unmet. These emotions can drive us to act on behaviors to replace those emotions with better feelings.

A child is no different, and can perceive any outcome that meets those needs as rewards. Anything that rewards the child for the behavior will reinforce the behavior and cause the

Examples of perceived rewards

- Non-action from the parent can be seen as a reward if it allows the child to continue what he wants to do, avoiding a consequence
- Avoiding yelling, arguing, or violence in the home
- A smile, giggle, or laugh
- Food or other small tokens (stickers, toys, candy, gum, points, or stars)
- Time with the parent
- Meeting any need that the child may perceive as previously unmet
- Public recognition of good behavior or achievements

child to continue until a better reward is available or a negative outcome occurs. Your non-action as a parent can be seen by the child as a positive outcome if it allows her to continue doing what she wants to do. A child who lives in a family environment with a lot of yelling, arguing, or violence could perceive a reward that avoids any of that and will look for and act on behaviors to meet that outcome.

Some parents confuse a positive reinforcement with a reward. A reward is something that is given to someone for doing something good, usually with the hope that the person will continue to do the good behavior. **Positive reinforcement can sometimes support bad or unwanted behavior.**

For example, if your child seeks attention in school, he may do something to make his classmates laugh. The laughter acts as positive reinforcement that will likely lead to him continuing to act out in class to make the class laugh.

Even something as simple as a smile or laugh will reinforce the behavior, even if the behavior is not positive. Farting is something that a lot of parents see as funny when it happens, but most parents probably don't want to reinforce a child farting in a restaurant or at school, or any place where the behavior could have negative consequences. It is important that parents be careful to not reinforce the unwanted behavior at restaurants or school, and teach the child when and where it is alright to fart.

The following table contains some examples of children's behaviors and the correlating needs and rewards from appropriate:

Need	Behavior	Parent's reaction	Perceived reward
Any number of reasons	Tantrum	Engaging the tantrum, yelling, or spanking	Get to spend time with mom or dad
Any number of reasons	Tantrum	Disengaging, calmly redirecting after the tantrum	Get to spend time with mom or dad
Belonging	Leaving bed after bedtime	Proactive time spent with kids before bedtime	Get to spend time with mom or dad
Belonging	Leaving bed after bedtime	Fixing a snack after bedtime	Get to spend time with mom or dad
Esteem	Intellectual power struggle (usually with teens)	Engaging in argument	Power struggle = respect from parents
Esteem	Intellectual power struggle	Disengaging from argument, redirection	Conversation = respect from parents

Notice that a parent can manage the same behavior differently, and produce the same reward, creating the opportunity for the parent to teach the child more manageable behaviors.

Negative to positive

Take a quick inventory of exactly how many negative parenting communications are used, including body language and sarcasm, versus positive parenting feedback. Most parents will be shocked to observe and learn the actual amount of negative communication they make with their children every day. It could be as simple as reactively snapping at a child's annoying, imperfect, or "not fast enough" behaviors.

The best place to start in improving with the skill of strategic praise is to examine any areas of negative parenting or dysfunctional communications that need to stop on our part first. **Then you can look at the different types of praise that fit your personality style and comfort.**

Determine what your triggers are, and whether or not you react negatively or positively. If you can plan on those triggers to continue to occur until changes are made, and learn how to not react to those triggers, implementing strategic praise will be easier. This is called **disengaging**, which we covered earlier in the workbook.

The purpose of using strategic praise is to change a behavior. What is actually happening is that the parent is **decreasing the bad behavior by disengaging from it, and then increasing the wanted behavior by rewarding and praising it.**

After you correct your own reactions to triggers, the next step in using this skill is to examine the family's values and goals and target the specific things that you want your child to learn, or the behaviors that you want to change.

Timing is everything
- Try to focus on only 3 – 5 target goals at a time, encouraging through consistency. You don't want the child to feel overwhelmed.
- Try to praise as soon as you see the good behavior, to make it easier to connect the behavior to the reward.
- The first few times that you see the target behavior, you should exaggerate your praise. When we say exaggerate, we mean EXAGERATE! Make it known that your child did something good, and that you like it! This increases the probability that your child will do the same behavior time after time.

Short and sweet, sweet being the important thing here
- Be excited that your child did something good, remember – Strategic Praise is a reward
- Praise with statements that assume the behavior and goal have been accomplished
- Avoid lecturing when praising, keep the praise directed at the good behavior. A reward is supposed to be enjoyable, and lectures and speeches are never enjoyable to a child.
- Your praise statements should be brief and, as often as appropriate, worded in the past as if they have already been achieved.

Your praise statements should be brief and, as often as appropriate, worded in the past as if they have already been achieved. If we continually state a goal in the future our minds perceive it as always being something we are working towards, but never achieve. You might recognize this pattern in your own goals.

If we want our children to visualize their accomplishment of the goal we need to word it in the past with faith that it will and has happened. This is an excellent opportunity for you to occasionally add your support of their bigger picture changes as they achieve baby steps towards their goals.

For example, "Hey you did it, that looks great, you're really starting to grow up into such a gentleman," or "Your homework looks great, I can see a definite difference in your attention to all of the details, it's excellent, your best yet, you keep surpassing yourself and your on your way to those goals for college you set." Remember to praise with support of the greater value only on occasion, otherwise it will appear that you are trying too hard or insincere.

Use generalized statements of the long-term life values to increase identity integration of the new behaviors.

Write down your long-term, values regarding the meaning of your life, your family and the lives of your children. This task is important in allowing us to discover that many of our day to day frustrations and how we handle them differs from our long-term hopes and dreams for our children. Certainly we want our children to be responsible, successful, moral and happy. I have found, in working with children for so many years that the value of being happy is actually intrinsic to success in the other value areas. Conversely I have worked with many parents who are struggling with their own depression, pessimism and negative relationships and don't realize those effects on the child's school failure, negative social skills or low motivation.

Rewards comes in different shapes

Prepare a daily, weekly or monthly incentive system that challenges the child's limits without overwhelming them to give up, prepare easy and immediate incentives to randomly reward attempts of the target behavior.

Every child is different and regardless of their intelligence they may need more immediate praise, incentives and rewards to focus through a difficult behavior change. If you are serious about changing a problem behavior you should prepare praise and incentives on a daily, weekly and monthly timeline.

This goals and rewards should be prepared with the child. Then, focus mainly on the daily tasks, since most children and even adults struggle to accomplish goals in the immediate moment of getting it done now. Even through the weekly and monthly accomplishments should be rewarded with planned incentives to teach children the results of patient perseverance; the real effectiveness of praise and incentives is immediately following the target behavior.

For example, you might develop a daily incentive of allowance, extra curfew, cell phone privileges, video game or TV time, or extra time with friends once their target task is complete. This is the daily, immediate motivator which dominates the view of children's motivations much more than even an extraordinary reward which might be several months away.

- **Food incentives:** most parents try to keep healthy food incentives, and there are always alternatives to "junk food." A lot of snacks are being made with healthier ingredients, some snacks are coming in "sugar-free" options, and there are many snacks made with real fruit. A lot of parents keep these things readily available.

- **Token systems** require some maintenance, and always have to be supported with real rewards that the child can get by trading in the tokens. It can be harder to use tokens than other rewards, because there will be learning opportunities when you're out of the house with the child – away from the goodie jar, star chart, or point system at home. When used effectively, though, **the child can earn valued rewards over time, teaching the child delayed gratification**, an important skill for school and work.

- **Privileges:** children always want to play with friends, play video games, talk on the phone, etc. Use that to your advantage in preparing effective reinforcers. Prepare easy and immediate incentives to randomly reward attempts of the target behavior immediately after it is completed.

- **Social reinforcers** include Strategic Praise, conversation, affection, and attention, and are readily available, and they require very little maintenance. These are probably the most effective reinforcers for parents, because they generally tend to reward a behavior and build the relationship at the same time.

- **Removal reinforcers** aren't usually used within behavior modification, because they usually involve removing painful or annoying things after a behavior. An example of this would be feeding a crying baby. When the baby begins to cry because he is hungry, the parent feeds the baby, removing that hunger.

One child may need creative praise or reward every 15 minutes for a target goal. Another child may need a weekly praise or reward every week because of their high level of self-discipline on that goal. Even the same child might need much more support and positives around a certain area of their life, like homework, but needs no support on eating healthy.

Keep the carrot of praise and rewards just outside of their "challenging zone" to push them with a focus on accomplishment of baby steps vs. failure of the bigger goal. This quality of creating the praise, rewards and carrots to fit the needs of the child is essential. Children who have a failure cycle require more positives. Once their self-discipline, self-esteem and self-accomplishment change, the positives can, and should, be smaller and less often.

The effects of affection

Strategic Praise has two qualities that anchor it as the most effective reward and create long-lasting relationship patterns: affection and quality one-on-one time. These aspects of Strategic Praise raise it to a level of significant positive relationship building, where **the child can feel the connection of a caring relationship through affection and valued one-on-one time.**

Affection is characterized by loving remarks, appropriate touching, and conversations that are exclusive to the parent and child. Affection expresses care, warmth, and love, and is the best way to build the relationship and sidestep problems.

Affection & Quality Time

Affection
- Loving remarks, appropriate touching, and unique conversations
- Being playful, silly, happy
- Ex.: tickling, games, reading time

Quality time
- One-on-One
- Time spent doing things the child enjoys
- Good time for affection
- Ex.: going out to dinner, reading time, going to the library

The more warmth and love that is felt in the relationship, the more the child is willing to do whatever the parent expects.

Affection is best served in **one-on-one time,** quality time spent with just the parent and child. In families with more than one child, try to create opportunities where you can be alone with one child every once in a while. Use that opportunity to be playful, silly, and affectionate. Those qualities communicate that the child is important and they carry that through their peer and dating relationships. That might also apply to your marriage or close friendships. The goal is to **create a relationship where your child will be willing to follow you anywhere and do anything you want, which is best done through affection and quality time.**

The "My teen, the lawyer" Exercise

Adolescents are looking for respect from the world, and will usually "fit in" better in places where they feel they are respected. In places where they are not feeling respected, they may do things that they think will give them power.

One example of this is the "Intellectual argument," where the teen will engage someone in an argument, regardless of his own position in the argument. Power is the main objective in this case, but the teen could also be looking for other rewards:

- Distracting the adult from a different problem
- Respect from peers ("I stood up to the adult!")
- Hoping the adult will give in to a reward for stopping the argument

1. You're not *just* trying to stop the argument. You're trying to teach the teen that there are better ways to earning power and respect

2. Determine the appropriate reward, teens usually want respect

3. Prepare yourself to DISENGAGE from the argument as soon as you see it start. Use a Calm Tone and say, "I respect that you have your opinions, and I think that's great. But, I don't want to have a debate with you. I'd be willing to talk about something else, though."

4. Find something else to do, but stay within sight of the teen. Wait patiently for her to talk about something else.

5. When she does come to you with something else, have a good conversation with the teen, maintaining a position of respect for the independent opinion. Use your Strategic Praise statement at the end of the conversation:

   "Thank you so much for not starting a debate. I hope you know that I do respect your opinions, and that you don't have to debate with me. If you need something, just come to me and ask, and if I can help you out, I will."

Engaging in the argument validates the teen's power in that situation. You want your teen to make her own decisions and earn respect and power, but you want her to be assertive and open about her needs, not argumentative or passive-aggressive.

The "Trail of Moms" Exercise

Interrupting in general is bad for the communication process, breaking down people's desire to want to communicate, and creating feelings of contempt as a person struggles to express opinions, thoughts, ideas, or emotions.

Children usually interrupt conversations when they are seeking attention from the parents. Every parent has probably been in the middle of a conversation – in the store, at home, at the park, on the phone – when their child has suddenly interrupted with, "Mom, mom, mom, mom, mom, mom." The Trail of Moms can continue forever.

1. You're not *just* trying to stop the Trail of Moms. You're trying to teach the child to not interrupt, and to wait until you are done talking.

2. The reward that the child is looking for is YOUR ATTENTION. You don't have to prepare any other reward. This one is easy.

3. Prepare yourself to IGNORE the child when she starts the Trail of Moms. This is a perfect time to use the Disengaging skill.

4. Stop your conversation, and using a Calm Tone, tell the child, "I'm in a conversation right now, so I need you be patient and not interrupt. Thanks." And then continue your conversation, even if there is nothing else to say – make up something.

5. When you finish your conversation, use your Strategic Praise statement:

   > "Thank you so much for being patient and not interrupting my conversation. It's important to be patient because it's nice to not interrupt and it's a way of showing someone that you're a big kid. I'm so glad you know how to do that. Since you didn't interrupt and let me finish my conversation, I can pay all my attention to you now."

If the parent engages in a conversation with the child when the child begins the trail of moms, just to get the child to stop interrupting, we are positively reinforcing the behavior.

Look at it this way: the child is actually reinforcing your behavior – stopping what you're doing to engage in a conversation with him – which is negatively reinforcing your behavior.

The child may interrupt again, or may try to negotiate, "But I just wanted to tell you…" You don't have to engage – go back to ignoring. Trust the process, because it does work, and it also teaches the child the more abstract idea that interrupting is not a good way of communicating.

Chapter 4 - Effective Reinforcement

Parenting Empowerment

Topics in this chapter

The Meaning of Life

Empowering vs. Enabling

What words do you use to empower your child?

Locus of control

Parenting Empowerment

The Meaning of Life – Raising your child to be an adult

The Parenting Paradox: How do you protect your child from the world, and let your child be independent at the same time?

Empowering good, Enabling baaaad
- Empower your child to be independent and to solve her own problems
- Avoid enabling – being over-protective, swooping in to rescue your child when there are problems.

How do you word it? What do you say to empower your child?

The Fallacy of Fatherhood – DAD, stop problem-solving, be affectionate!

Locus of control – a leading factor in school achievement
- Internal locus of control: child believes that his actions affect his situation
- External locus of control: child believes that what he does doesn't matter, so why even try?

Encourage your child: **"You can do it yourself"** and **"I need you to solve the problem."**

The Meaning of Life

This section of the book might get a little sappy. But, we'd like to talk about the meaning of life for a bit.

In our busy lives, we don't usually have time to ponder the meaning of life, although it may pop into our minds on a daily commute, or a boring night at home, or watching a child learn something new that totally amazes us. Any thought on the subject usually involves a higher being, or a cosmic plan that was created for human kind, and doesn't usually consider the blessings we see every day.

> Our purpose as parents, our meaning of life, is to raise our children to be adults. It's a paradox – we're supposed to invest all of this time, money, emotion, and energy into raising a child that is going to end up leaving us.

But, if we step back and look at the big picture of what our purpose is as parents, we can come to at least this conclusion: Our purpose as parents, our meaning of life, is to raise our children to be adults.

It's a paradox – we're supposed to invest all of this time, money, emotion, and energy into raising a child that is going to end up leaving us. AND, we're supposed to be happy about that? Some of the greatest moments in our lives - the little league games, the antics at the dinner table, the holiday fun - are brought to us by our children on a daily basis for decades, and then they leave us.

The Parenting Paradox

The paradox of parenting is the balance that parents have to maintain between the natural act of protecting the child from problems, bad people, and serious consequences for actions and the need for the child to become independent, learn coping skills, and learn how to solve his own problems.

The act of protecting the child is a natural, animal instinct, built into the innate – almost survival – needs of every living being. The mama bird protects her nest; hunting lion prides hide their cubs in the long grasses; the kangaroo jill stashes joey in her pouch.

However, **it is also important that children become independent**, developing their own values, becoming significant members of the community, learning skills to help them meet goals and establish their own lives. Baby birds learn to fly, lion cubs hunt, and the joey learns to leap.

Both acts are necessary to the survival and happiness of the child. While we may feel healthy and indestructible when we are young, most parents also naturally begin speculating their own mortality. It's natural – humans consider life along with death – and also begin planning. Health insurance, life insurance, death insurance all have new meaning when we have kids. We start to prepare for the care of our families, in case we become disabled or die, **which makes an even-more prominent case for raising a child to be independent**.

Balancing the protectiveness and the independence is a skill that has to be learned, like anything else. It involves learning when to teach and when to hold back, effective communication and setting boundaries, and most importantly parents have to know how to push their children to grow.

Empowering vs. Enabling

Enabling is described in research as protecting a person from natural consequences to his behavior. A lot of research has been done in schools and juvenile justice studying parents who enable their children, preventing schools and the court systems from effectively treating and consequencing kids for doing unwanted behaviors or breaking the law.

Empowering means exactly the opposite, referring to parents who push their child to solve her own problems and to assume power over her own life and situations. Empowering parents will let the child experience consequences for behaviors, whether good or bad, to help the child learn by experiences.

> **Empowering vs. Enabling**
>
> **Empowering:** encouraging your child to solve her own problems and make her own decisions
>
> **Enabling:** solving problems for your child, "covering for him," buying his way out of trouble," failing to follow through with consequences

Basically, empowering a child teaches her to make her own decisions, solve her own problems, and learn how to ask for help. The empowering parent doesn't hover over the child, allows the child to make mistakes, and pushes the child to learn new things.

The enabling parent hovers over the child, and is often overbearing, overprotective, and doesn't allow anyone, especially the school and court system to give the child consequences for behaviors. This teaches the child to learn how to lie, manipulate the system, and that the parent will always fix problems.

ENABLING

A parent who is enabling is usually overprotective, over-bearing, and constantly hovering over the child with the intention of protecting the child. **Some characteristics of an enabling parent include:**

- Covering for the child, "buying his way out of trouble"
- **Attitude of "I'll do it for you" and "Don't worry about it, I'll take care of it."**
- "Giving in" when the child begins crying, usually buying the toy or candy that the child is screaming for
- **Making excuses for the child, blaming others for the child's situation**
- Making the school change
- Making others unreasonably accommodate the child (through force or manipulation)
- Sometimes a parent will lie to cover for a child

These are some of the more extreme **examples** that we've seen of parents enabling their child:

- We've seen cases where the parent allows the child to stay home from school because he says he's tired. Some cases have had more than 100 absences in a school year.
- Parents claimed that the child didn't do homework, because she had to baby sit while mom was at a friend's house.
- Enabling parents will do homework for the child, giving answers and solutions
- We've seen parents claim that the school system is at fault when the child receives bad grades.
- We've seen false accusations of discrimination, assault, and physical and sexual harassment.

When the parent enables the child, the child learns:
- She can manipulate a situation to get what she wants
- He can lie to get what he wants
- That others control situations when she gets into trouble, and that she can't do anything to fix the problem
- Mom or dad will keep him out of trouble, no matter what he does
- People "owe" her something, even if for no reason, and they should accommodate her with whatever she asks

Some examples of a child manipulating a situation to get what he wants include:
- Having a tantrum in a store to get candy or a toy
- Acting sick to stay home from school
- Playing one parent against the other
- Making excuses for not doing school work

EMPOWERING

A parent who empowers the child is the exact opposite of the enabling parent – consistent when enforcing rules, allows space so the child can experience new things, and engages the child in healthy discussion about a problem that the child is having, . **Some characteristics of an empowering parent include:**

- **Does not always step in when a child has a problem**, teaches the child to ask for help, will only intervene when the child asks for help
- **Encourages: "You can do it" and "I need you to problem-solve."**
- Doesn't "give in" when the child tantrums or argues, uses the "poker face"
- Helps the child problem-solve, instead of making excuses for the child
- Discourages blaming others, making excuses, manipulating, and lying
- Does not overreact when the child falls, cries, or gets hurt
- Helps the child find ways to accommodate the situation, to find solutions
- Always teaching the child that honesty is a great value

These are some **examples** that we've seen of parents empowering their child:

- We've seen cases where the child has broken the law, is taken to the juvenile detention center, and eventually ordered to appear at court, and the parent will make sure that the child accomplishes the requirements that consequences entail. The parent is sympathetic, but also teaches the child that he has to deal with his own consequences.
- During homework sessions, the parent will not do the homework for the child, and will maintain a poker face when the child is learning new skills. Some kids learn to read the parents face, and will guess at the homework answers, until the parent's facial expression tells her that she is correct.

When the parent empowers the child, the child learns:
- She can solve her own problems
- He can make his own decisions
- She learns how to problem-solve, how to get people to help her, and important social skills to be able to communicate and build relationships
- The child learns 'delayed gratification,' meaning that she can do the good behavior when the reward will come later or the reward may never come at all
- Most importantly: the child learns to control his impulses, learns that rewards will come for doing good things, and that his behavior affects his own situation more than any other factors

Some small examples of how empowering a child will affect the child:
- Learning to dress himself and get ready for school in the morning
- The child learns to meet her own needs and will ask for help when she needs it
- Able to pay attention in school and exhibit appropriate behaviors
- Reading and math success depend on parent participation and empowerment

There is a way to communicate with your child to empower your child to make his own decisions, called the **Empowering Conversation.**

The Empowering Conversation

7. **Problem Statement**: Kid – "Billy made fun of me today. I started to cry and then everyone made fun of me."

8. **Empathy Statement**: Parent – "Well that stinks. I bet you felt really bad about them laughing."

9. **Behavior Statement**: Kid – "Yeah, I was so mad, that I punched Billy, and now the teacher wants to talk to you."

10. **Empowerment Statement**: Parent – "So what are you going to do about this problem?"

11. **Problem-Ownership Statement**
Kid – "I don't know, what do I do?"

12. **Advice Statement**: Parent – Explain the options, with possible rewards and consequences

The empathy statement is how the parent verbally expresses impartiality, showing that the child doesn't have to feel guilty, even if he feels mad or sad. This is important to the process in that oftentimes, guilt or shame will lead to anxiety, nervousness, or depression, which can cause a person to shut down and not solve problems.

Once the parent gives help or advice without the child's consent, the parent has taken back the power from the child. **If you offer help or advice, and the child doesn't want it, let it go! DISENGAGE!** If the child does want advice, remind the child that you are not telling the child what to do, and that all you are doing is offering some advice.

In the problem-ownership statement, the child should be able to acknowledge that it is her problem, and she will have to take responsibility and deal with any consequences. Most kids are smart, they know how to work their way through problems. It is the role of the parent to help the child find a healthy plan.

What words do you use to empower your child?

Believe it or not, there is a conversation style that a parent can use to empower the child. We call it the Empowering Conversation.

There are six steps in the Empowering Conversation, each having its own purpose, but all working toward the same goal: advising, helping, and teaching the child to take ownership for solving his own problems.

Ownership means that someone assumes ultimate responsibility of something. A car owner has the responsibility of maintenance, insurance, and licensing. A business owner has the responsibility of paying employees and other bills, ensuring safety in work conditions and use of any products that are sold, etc.

Ownership also means that the "owner" can also reap the rewards that come from those responsibilities. A car owner can drive to work, a friend's house, go out on a date. A business owner gets the profit from the business.

It is important to teach the child that she can make her own decisions, but that she has to be okay with whatever reward or responsibility that may come with the decision. It is also important that the parent remain calm and non-judgmental through the entire process. If the child senses anger, fear, or anxiety from the parent, she may "shut down." She will also avoid talking to the parent about problem in the future, because she will remember that the last problem made Mom mad or sad or whatever emotion that was perceived.

Remember – kids don't have the same amount of experience as parents, and need to be coached; but at the same time, parents should not solve problems for the child. **The Empowering Conversation works through a problem with the child as a learning process, which may require some coaxing.**

1. The problem statement is the way in which the child will present the problem, including a description and his feelings about the problem. The parent should be careful not to overreact when the child presents the problem – remember the poker face.

In a calm tone, the parent should coax as much information as possible from the child. Use active listening skills, be attentive and patient as the child talks, and remove all the barriers to communication – remember, the little things count the most. Some examples include:

- Stop eating and put down your fork
- Pull over the car so you can listen better
- Turn off the TV
- Sit down with the child – you don't have to be in any particular position, but make sure that the interaction is non-threatening or judgmental

2. The empathy statement is the next step in the conversation, where the parent verbally expresses impartiality, showing that the child doesn't have to feel guilty, even if he feels mad or sad. This is important to the process in that oftentimes, guilt or shame will lead to anxiety, nervousness, or depression, which can cause a person to shut down and not solve problems.

This step is an expression of empathy from the parent, because the parent has probably experienced what the child is going through, and will be able to relate to the emotions and attitudes. There will be times, especially in our quickly-changing world, where the parent will not be able to relate to the child's problem, but can show sympathy for the situation. By maintaining a non-judgmental, learning experience, the parent will be able to show empathy in the problem-solving process.

3. The behavior statement is the third stage, where the child should pinpoint the specific problem-behavior and link it to both the immediate and delayed consequences. This requires the parent to help the child through the critical thinking process, showing how one thing cause another, which causes another, and then another.

Be careful that you don't lecture the child. Use a tone that sounds like a teacher who is explaining something, rather than a parent who is scolding. Eventually, the child will be able to do the critical thinking on his own, even linking behaviors to consequences before he acts.

4. The empowerment statement allows the parent to transfer power in this situation to the child. In a very

> The empathy statement is how the parent verbally expresses impartiality, showing that the child doesn't have to feel guilty, even if he feels mad or sad.
>
> This is important to the process in that oftentimes, guilt or shame will lead to anxiety, nervousness, or depression, which can cause a person to shut down and not solve problems.

subtle way, reinforce that it is good that the child is concerned and is trying to work his way through the problem.

In this stage of the conversation, the parent should express to the child that it is her problem to deal with, and then offer to help if it seems like the child is struggling. You don't want the child to struggle so much that he shuts down, so be encouraging.

Use empowering statements, such as:
- "What are you going to do about it?"
- "Do you want some advice?"
- "Do you want to know what I did when I was your age?"
- "What are your options?"

5. In the problem-ownership statement, the child should be able to acknowledge that it is her problem, and she will have to take responsibility and deal with any consequences. Most kids are smart, they know how to work their way through problems. It is the role of the parent to help the child find a healthy plan.

The child may express that he doesn't know what to do, and the parent should reinforce that it is okay to be unsure, but also revert back to the empowerment statement.

The child: "I don't know what to do" or "I don't know how."

The parent: "That sounds like a tough situation. That happened to me once, do you want to know what I did?"

> If you offer help or advice, and the child doesn't want it, let it go! DISENGAGE!
>
> If the child does want advice, remind the child that you are not telling the child what to do, and that all you are doing is offering some advice.

Very important note: if you offer help or advice, and the child doesn't want it, LET IT GO! DISENGAGE! Keep the door open, so that the child can come back to you if he decides to, but do not keep pressing the situation. Once the parent gives help or advice without the child's consent, the parent has taken back the power from the child.

The child: "I don't know what to do" or "I don't know how."

The parent: "That sounds like a tough situation. Let me know if you want some advice," or "That's tough. Come and find me if you need some help figuring it out."

6. The advice statement is where the parent is allowed to help, after being given permission from the child. Reinforce the child for asking for help – being able to get someone to help is very important to a person's self-esteem, and is linked to academic and job success. Remind the child that you are not telling him what to do, and that all you are doing is offering some advice.

Also, maintain child's position of power, by projecting yourself into her situation. This will maintain the non-judgmental tone of the conversation, and keep open the lines of communication for future problems.

It is better to know that the child is having a problem, than to have him hide the problem from you. Kids will often do that if they think that the parent will be mad. This leads to lies and manipulation, not just in childhood or adolescence, but also into adulthood.

The child: "Yeah, can you help me?"

The parent: "I would love to help you! Thanks for asking. Here is what I would do if I was in your situation…." or "What I did when I had the same problem was to…"

The fallacy of fatherhood

Research supports many of the assumptions that underlie our societal norms. For example, dads are more likely to empower a child, while moms are more likely to coddle, which supports the adage that a child will run to mom when there's a problem, because she will fix it. The adage assumes that dad won't fix it, but will make the child fix the problem through problem-solving efforts, or accept the consequences.

> **We have seen a lot of fathers treat the child's problems like they are work problems, brainstorming and decision-making.**

This is not an altogether unhealthy dynamic, but it depends on several factors:

1. The dad has to be able to be nurturing and affectionate at least part of the time, because there will be problems that can't be fixed through problem-solving, such as a scraped knee, or hurt feelings (wounded ego). In those situations, the parent has to be able to nurture the child through empathy, not problem-solving.

2. Similarly, mom has to be able to stop nurturing at times, and push the child to problem-solve. The child has to learn that that both parents want the child to be independent, and at the same time can be affectionate and nurturing, tending to their feelings. There should be times where promoting independence is more important than temporary emotions.

3. Also, mom and dad have to be able to communicate with each other about the child's problems and how they should be handled. The family dynamic changes if both parents coddle the child, or if both parents are always in problem-solving mode.

The fallacy of fatherhood is that men expect men to be manly, and aren't usually openly nurturing when in public or in the presence of male friends. Men expect other men to be problem-solvers, to empower their children to be independent, rather than coddle and be affectionate.

We have seen a lot of fathers treat the child's problems like they are work problems, brainstorming and decision-making. Also, fathers tend to believe that teaching a child to solve problems involves lectures, yelling, criticizing - behaviors that the father may have learned from his own father. These behaviors are largely ineffective, because they breakdown the communication process. Think how you may have felt with the "When I was your age" speech.

Mothers also have to be problem-solvers. Admittedly, it is very hard to not be nurturing or coddling when a child has a problem. Research has shown that children have to be empowered in order for the child to learn that he has the ability to make decisions and solve problems. **Parents have to be able to refrain from enabling children, and use problems as learning opportunities.** This is important for the child's development in several ways:

- There is a connection between empowerment and internal locus of control.
- There is a connection between enabling and external locus of control.
- Locus of control affects school achievement, work ethic, and potential career opportunities.

> Some problems can't be solved, and **Dad** has to be able to nurture the child through empathy, not problem-solving.
>
> **Mom** has to be able to stop nurturing at times, and push the child to problem solve.

Parents as coaches, teachers, consultants, and confidantes

The role of the parent will change as the child ages and begins to assume new values, goals, and motivations for behaviors. Three primary age groups that we want to discuss are the Infant/toddler, childhood, and adolescence.

In the early stages of child development, the parent is a life-line, helping the child meet survival and safety needs. Anyone who has had a toddler knows that there is a potential for danger in every room in the house and at the edge of every table and counter top, and worries about the child wandering off in the store as the child discovers the physical world.

In the early stages, the parent is the protector, provider, and play toy. The child uses the parent for everything from food and shelter to lifeguard and nurse, from a food bag to an exercise gym.

Age group	Motivations	Parenting style
Infant/toddler	Discovering the physical world; needs are more physical (survival) and safety needs; the child develops trust, but also uses the parent to meet needs	Protector, Provider, and Play toy
Childhood	Discovering his role in the world; learns to develop friendships and the rules of interaction; takes on the parent's values as his own	Role model, Teacher, Coach, Therapist
Adolescence	Peer interaction is often more important than family; don't want to be lectured or judged; will meet needs outside of the home	Consultant, Advisor, Confidante, Friend

Childhood, between the ages of 3 and 12, is the time where the child discovers his role in the world, how he fits in within the family dynamic, and how to get along with other kids. The parent's role in this stage is that of a teacher, coach, therapist, and the source of trust and love. In this stage, the child will develop deep-seated, long-lasting values and views of the world, and it is important that the parent help guide those values by being a role model.

Children between ages 3-5 will test boundaries and may tantrum to see how far they can push people, but this is a natural act in the learning process. Testing the limits of our actions is how we learn norms, rules, and boundaries. Parents have to be patient during these years, and practice The Calm Tone, Effective Reinforcement, and Empowerment skills.

In adolescence, EVERYTHING CHANGES. Many parents don't realize that the changes in their adolescent require that the parent also change parenting tactics. In this stage, the parent has to transition into the role of the consultant, advisor, confidante, and friend. Teenagers are very concerned with "fitting in" with their peers, and will even assume the same values, likes, dislikes, and behaviors. This is a natural process.

The consultant style requires that the parent use the Empowering Conversation in EVERY conversation. Most adolescents don't want to feel judged, lectured, or limited, and may avoid conversations if the parent is going to cause those feelings. At the same time, the adolescent is looking for respect from peers, trying to fit in with peers.

The adolescent stage is also where the teenager begins learning about romantic relationships. The parent can either choose to guide that natural process by befriending the adolescent, or the parent can push away the teenager, by not changing the parenting style.

Most teenagers are looking for acceptance and esteem in this stage, and will find ways to meet those needs, even in unhealthy ways or outside of the home. **Parents who don't use the Empowering Conversation with their adolescent may experience extreme behaviors**, as the adolescent tries to exert his power and independence. Some of these extreme behaviors can include:

- The adolescent not wanting to have any contact with the parent or go home
- Sneaking out to go to a boyfriend's house

- Having sex in order to feel loved
- Having unrealistic goals
- Allowing others to violate his values and goals in order to feel a sense of belonging
- Gang involvement/ Committing crimes
- Drug use as a way to maintain friendships

The point: remove the barriers that will make your teenager not want to communicate with you, or come home. Parenting an adolescent is similar to managing employees, the happier the employee, the more they'll want to come work.

Locus of control

Locus of control literally means the point of control. It is defined in research as one's belief in where the control and power over his life actually lies. A person's locus of control is generally described on a scale between external and internal. Although there are research-based tests to determine a person's locus of control, it is looked at as a scale, where people usually lean toward one direction or the other.

Locus of Control

External   Internal

The belief that you don't have any **power over your situation**, the things that happen to you are affected more by factors beyond yourself, such as other people, luck, or fate.	The belief that you have **power over your situation,** and that the things that happen to you are caused by your decisions and actions.
A person who believes that other people have more control over her life than she does may blame others when things go wrong, instead of problem-solving her way through the situation.	A person with an internal locus of control will usually problem-solve her way through situations, relying upon her own experiences, education, training, skills, and any help that she may be able to procure.

Problems with an External Locus of Control

External locus of control is one of the primary effects of the enabling parenting style and refers to a person's belief that he doesn't have any control over the things that happen to him. These things include consequences for behavior, grades, job opportunities, job pay, health issues, etc.

It is easier to see the problems that occur when a child has an external locus of control when the child enters his school-age years. As the child enters school and begins to have interaction with more people, both kids and adults, behavior patterns develop that are more noticeable to professionals, like teachers, counselors, and school administration.

Parenting style also becomes more noticeable, as the parent makes trips to the school to "bail out" their kid. The child learns to manipulate situations so that mom will have to go down to the school and bail out the kid, usually in an attempt to get attention. The child learns to meet needs, just like everyone else, but meets them in unhealthy ways.

Parenting style	Locus of Control	Characteristics of the child
Enabling	External	• Believes that **someone will "save" them** during problems • **Learns to manipulate, lie, or threaten**, instead of problem-solve and find solutions • Believes that external factors affect situations and outcomes, **instead of own behaviors** • Behaves impulsively, because **"what I do doesn't matter"**
Empowering	Internal	• **Personal**: Independence, resilience, healthy self esteem, impulse control • **School**: Concentration, increased attention span, delayed gratification • **Relationships**: able to say "NO," enforce boundaries and protect values • **Develops work ethic**, because "my behaviors affect my situation

If a child develops a sense that she has no control over his life, she is more likely to develop anxiety and depression. The child may experience lower academic achievement, fewer relationships, and negative consequences for behaviors. External locus of control is also associated with adolescent males with conduct disorder and delinquency in adolescent females. There are many serious outcomes that are associated with delinquency and conduct disorder, such as incarceration, teen pregnancy, drug and alcohol use, and poor school performance.

Basically, enabling causes the child to meet needs in unhealthy ways and eventually have fewer educational and job opportunities.

When does enabling work, when is it good?

Research has shown that enabling parents with graduate/Masters degree level education or training have children with the greatest level of internal locus of control. Studies have not identified the causes for this, but it most likely because those parents also have several positive characteristics that offset the effects of the enabling:

- **Role modeling** – Graduate level parents display the rewards of having a strong work ethic and education through the family's lifestyle and their own actions
- **Affection** – Interactions with kids are affectionate and loving,
- **Meaningful interaction** – Graduate level parents may not have more time with their kids, but they use the time for meaningful interaction
- **Communication with the child** is probably empowering, even though the parent may "rescue" the child from problems at school and other areas of life

The darker side of external locus of control

The following material is not meant to help diagnose your child or make a complete connection between locus of control and two mental health disorders. Instead, we are including the following to show that there is a connection between locus of control and common disorders in delinquent adolescents, and that those disorders can be disruptive to the child's and the family's lives. Oppositional defiant disorder (ODD) and conduct disorder (CD) are common mental health disorders for delinquent adolescents. According to the DSM IV, ODD is marked by the following characteristics:

1. Look for patterns that last 6 months or more, with negativistic, hostile, and defiant behaviors, with at least four of the following warning signs:
   a. Frequently loses temper
   b. Frequently argues with adults
   c. Frequently defies or refuses to comply with requests or rules made by adults, usually through active, aggressive, or passive-aggressive behaviors
   d. Frequently blames others for the consequences of his mistakes or misbehavior
   e. Is usually "touchy" or easily annoyed by others
   f. Can be frequently angry or resentful
   g. Can be frequently spiteful or vindictive
   h. The unhealthy behaviors cause significant harm in relationships, school, or work performance
2. The behaviors aren't symptoms of Psychotic or Mood Disorder, which would have to be diagnosed by a physician.
3. The behaviors aren't symptoms of Conduct Disorder, or Antisocial Personality Disorder if the person is 18 years or older.

   Conduct disorder (CD) is similar to ODD in nature of consistent patterns of unhealthy behaviors, but the CD child will actively seek to violate other people's boundaries, rights, and values. The behaviors of CD will usually be more aggressive, and has been linked to abusive parents, who may be diagnosable with Antisocial Personality Disorder, and have probably been arrested, incarcerated or show signs of alcohol or drug abuse. **Conduct Disorder is marked by the following characteristics:**

   A. The child exhibits a pattern of behaviors that violate the boundaries and basic human rights of others, or breaking age-appropriate norms or rules, with at least 3 of the following warning signs in the past 12 months, with at least one symptom present in the past 6 months.
      1. **Aggressive behaviors toward animals or other people**
         a. Bullies, threatens, or intimidates others
         b. Initiates fights
         c. Used a weapon with the potential for serious harm (gun, knife, bat, stick, etc)
         d. Physically cruel to people
         e. Physically cruel to animals
         f. Theft, with conflict with a victim (mugging, extortion, armed robbery)
         g. Forced sex (any sexual behavior by manipulation, threat, or aggression)
      2. **Destruction of property**
         a. Starting fires with the intent to cause serious damage

b. Other behaviors with the intent to cause serious property damage (tagging, destruction, shootings, etc)

3. **Deceit**
   a. Breaking into a house, building, car, or other property
   b. Frequently lies to others to get things or favors, or to avoid responsibilities ("cons people")
   c. Theft, without contact with a victim (shoplifting, forgery, etc)

4. **Serious behaviors that violate rules**
   a. Staying out after curfew set by parent, with patterns starting earlier than 13 years old
   b. Run away overnight at least twice (this symptom could include one run away incident if the child did not return for a lengthy period of time)
   c. School truancy, with patterns starting earlier than 13 years old

B. The unhealthy behaviors cause significant harm in relationships, school, or work performance.

C. The behaviors aren't symptoms of Conduct Disorder, or Antisocial Personality Disorder if the person is 18 years or older.

The severity of the disorder can range between mild, moderate, and severe depending on the amount and type of harm that is caused to others, and the number of incidents where the child has presented the symptoms of Conduct Disorder.

The "Getting Dressed" Exercise

Getting a four year old to dress himself in the morning and get ready for pre-school may seem daunting, but it is possible. It will be difficult in the beginning.

Kid: I don't want to get dressed; I want you to dress me.

Parent: It can be difficult to do things like big kids, but I think you can handle it. You do a lot of things without me.

Kid: Yeah, but I tried and I can't do it, I want you to dress me.

Parent: Well, I'm trying to get ready for work, and when I'm ready, we're going to go. I need you to get yourself ready by then. What do you need to do to get yourself ready?

Kid: Get out some pants, and a shirt, and socks.

Parent: That's a great start! I know you can do it. If you go put on pants, and a shirt, and socks, I'll help you tie your shoes.

The "Your teenager got a speeding ticket" Exercise

Kid: I got a speeding ticket on the way to school, and then I got in trouble at school because I was late

Parent: Well, that sucks, how fast were you going?

Kid: 15 over. I woke up late, and I was in a hurry. Now I have to stay after school, and I'll miss basketball practice and get benched.

Parent: Sounds like a tough situation. What are you going to do?

Kid: I don't know, I guess I should talk to my coach.

Parent: Do you want some advice?

Kid: No, I know what you're going to say – I need to get up earlier.

Parent: That would be good… and let me know if you need any help with the other stuff.

Discipline

Topics in this chapter

Why this chapter is only 2 pages long: see Chapters 3-5

Why doesn't punishment work?

Value Options – the secret weapon

Affection is pre-emptive

Discipline

USE DISCIPLINE & PUNISHMENT AS LITTLE AS POSSIBLE

Discipline should only include loss of privileges or retraining the child to do the good behaviors.

Types of discipline techniques that don't work:
- Lecturing
- Yelling
- Time-outs
- Ultimatums
- Removing tokens
- Physical discipline or punishment

Strategic praise, rewards, and effective communication work better than punishment

Value Options – the most effective discipline tactic

Affection and Play time prevent a lot of stress and need for discipline – get your child to *want* to follow your instructions!

Why this chapter is only 2 pages long: see Chapters 3-5

OK, this chapter is 10 pages long, but parents should at least read Chapters 3, 4 and 5, because parenting is less about discipline, and more about teaching. **You will spend a lot less time disciplining your children** if you can effectively communicate what you expect from them, and if you can be proactive using *Strategic Praise*.

Most parents relate discipline to some type of punishment, control tactic, or restraint in an attempt to establish authority. However, the word discipline actually comes from the word disciple, which means follower, believer, and even student. When we say 'discipline as little as possible,' we're actually referring to the common association with punishment.

This chapter will only offer one skill relating to discipline, Value Options, and it's not a form of punishment. Instead, it enforces boundaries and maintains the family's values by teaching the child to make good decisions. The rest of the chapter will discuss ways to avoid using discipline and punishment. Value Options is supported by all of the other skills in previous chapters. To use it effectively, you'll have to master The Calm Tone, disengaging, the empowering conversation, and effective reinforcement. This chapter will also provide the reasons why some other disciplinary techniques do not work.

> The word discipline actually comes from the word disciple, which means follower, believer, and even student, but most parents think of it as some type of punishment.

Why doesn't punishment work?

Your role as a parent is to get your child to do what you need him to do to grow, be happy, and contribute to the family. There are basically two ways to get your children to do what you want them to do: **there's the easy way, and there's the hard way.**

The easy way is through punishment, bickering, arguing, yelling, lecturing, or using any of the other negative communication skills. Punishment breaks down relationships and the communication process, causing the child to experience emotions related to fear, sadness, and anger, as they try to determine the reason why the parent is acting aggressively. **The worst type of punishment is physical, and should never be used in the home!**

The hard way is to use the skills that are outlined in the rest of this book. You want your kids to follow you willingly, not by force. Think about your job – would you work at a place where your boss criticizes you, punishing you when you make a mistake? Would you follow a leader that yells and argues? Value Options is the healthy alternative to punishment for kids who are having trouble seeing the rewards for doing healthy behaviors. In the long-run, the hard way will benefit the child so much more.

At work, when an employee breaks the rules, that employee is subject to many different types of consequences:

Consequences at your job:
- Verbal warning
- Written warning
- Training
- Loss of pay
- Demotion
- Termination
- Rearranging responsibilities

Notice that these consequences are warnings, loss of privileges, or trainings to better equip the employee to do the job. Obviously you can't fire your child from the family, but the systems for reacting to unwanted behaviors should be similar.

Things that should be privileges, not automatic:
- TV
- Movies
- Allowance
- Games & Toys
- Use of the car
- Use of the phone
- Going out with friends
- Going out to play

There are so many things that are readily available to use as reinforcers, either to reward a behavior or to apply a consequence by removing a privilege. Yet, parents continue to discipline the child in ways that are ineffective.

> **Discipline should only include loss of privileges or retraining the child to do the good behaviors. A lot of parents don't use privileges strategically, allowing the child to take things for granted that should be privileges.**

There are several reasons why most parents use discipline and punishment more than they should:
- They learned it from their parents
- It's easier to come up with a punishment than it is use proactive affection, Effective Reinforcement, Strategic Praise, and relationship-building.

- In the heat of the moment, it takes effort on the parent's part to remain calm and be patient
- Parenting requires that the parent role-model behaviors that they want the child to use, which can be hard to do
- **Too many rules** – some families have so many rules that the child is bound to break one

Ineffective discipline techniques:

Technique	Why the technique is ineffective
Lecturing	**You have a minute to keep your child's attention**, and that is only if the conversation is interactive. You have as long as a kids' cereal commercial to get your message across, even if you have cartoon characters helping you.
Yelling	**Completely breaks down the conversation**, as the child is more concerned with the fear that something bad is happening.
Time Out	Most parents use Time Out for extensive periods of time, usually longer than expected, and then the child gets bored and begins testing the parent. Time Out should only be used to deescalate the situation – **see Chapter 2 on Disengaging.**
Ultimatums	You can't feasibly follow through with every ultimatum. Also, ultimatums are aggressive in nature, and the child will pick up that aggression, and will probably use it at school.
Removing tokens	Too much maintenance – parenting should be easier than that. Tokens can also be a problem for rewarding a behavior, because they are not always available, and there has to be bigger rewards tied to the tokens.
Spanking	**Completely breaks down the conversation**, as the child is more concerned with the fear that something bad is happening. **Physical punishment also breaks down the relationship.**

Set up some simple rules based on your family's value set, we recommend less than 10.
- Keep the rules simple and general
- Relate the rules to bigger concepts
- Ex: Be honest, Use a Calm Tone, Be respectful
- You don't even have to write them down, as long as you assert them as the family's values

Let your child break the rules to teach him boundaries
- You don't have to hover over child to prevent him from breaking the rules. It's bound to happen, that's how children learn.

- It's actually not healthy to hover over your child (see Chapter 4 – Parenting Empowerment)
- Let your child learn from experience! There are only a few things that parents should really be worried about: sex, drugs, and criminal conduct, and if your relationships in the home are healthy, you probably won't even have to worry about those things!
- **Teach the child when he does break the rules, don't punish or criticize.**

Your discipline strategy should try to be an immediate intervention to stop and correct the inappropriate behavior. Catching the behavior in the act is the best time to correct the behavior. When the discipline can't be immediate, your communication style has to take over to take the child back to the incident.

We'd like to emphasize the importance of reinforcing wanted behaviors, because they work for both short-term and long-term issues. We couldn't write enough about Effective Reinforcement, because it is the healthiest way to parent. The discipline

> **You have to give 100% of your energy to using Effective Reinforcement in order to expect any kind of behavior changes in your family.**

technique that we teach in this chapter, Value Options, should be used sparingly, and only in situations where you've tried everything else.

Value Options – the secret weapon

Value Options should be the only discipline technique you use, if you're also using Effective Reinforcement. You have to give 100% of your energy to using Effective Reinforcement in order to expect any kind of behavior changes in your family. Value Options requires that the parent be proficient in all of the skills in this workbook.

We should emphasize that this is the best tactic for discipline. However, the parent can also use Value Options in any situation, because it empowers the child while maintaining some sense of the family's values. The lectures, time outs, anger, and other punishments just don't work.

Step #1: Assess the situation

Take a second to ignore your child, and assess the situation to determine your needs and the child's needs. What is motivating the child's behavior? This is an important question, because children don't often have the vocabulary to clearly assert their wants, needs, and values. You have to be careful that you are not trying to correct a behavior that may be caused by something as simple as hunger or fatigue.

On the other hand, you should also assess your own needs, to make sure that you're not misperceiving the behavior, simply because you're tired or hungry. Check your 3P's from the Effective Reinforcement process, and implement a plan that you already have in place. Answer these questions:

> **What behavior do you want to see happen RIGHT NOW?**
> **What can you use to reward that behavior if it happens?**
> **What behavior do you NOT want to see right now?**
> **Will the child value the reward that your're willing to give?**

Value Options

Step #1: Assess the situation

- Check your 3 P's
- What are your needs?
- What need is the child trying to meet?

Step #2: Set the scene

During a severe problem-behavior situation, the parent has to use the following skills in order to effectively use Value Options.

- De-escalate the situation:
  5. Use The Calm Tone
  6. Check your Non-Verbal communication
  7. Check your attitude
  8. Disengage

- Strategic Praise
- Parenting Empowerment
- Empathy
- Affection

Step #3: Offer 2 options

- **Option 1: the wanted behavior and the reward**
- **Option 2: the unwanted behavior WITHOUT the reward**
- Make sure the options are things that you can follow-through with – be realistic
- Teach your child about rewards and consequences for decisions

Step #4: Follow-through with the child's decision

- You have to follow through with the decision, you can't turn back
- State the consequences as you follow through
- Allow the child to change his mind
- Use *The Calm Tone*

Use Strategic Praise after your follow-through, praising the child for making a good decision, and for using a Calm Tone. "That was a great decision! I'm so glad that you figured out how to do that, and you did it on your own! And we didn't have to argue or get loud about it – we solved it using a Calm Tone. Thank you so much."

Step #2: Set the scene

Don't try to take control of the situation, you'll only be engaging in a power struggle, even if there wasn't a power struggle. **Your job in this step is to de-escalate the situation, and then regroup.** During a severe problem-behavior situation, the parent has to use the following skills in order to effectively use Value Options.

To de-escalate the situation, use the skills taught earlier in this book:

1. **The Calm Tone** – the louder the child gets, the more calm you should get. Also, remember that your tone of voice and intonation can affect the message to the child. You don't want to sound authoritative or critical – sound calm.
2. **Non-Verbal communication** – make sure your non-verbals are non-threatening and don't express authority. Bend down to the child's eye level and use your poker face
3. **Check your attitude** – emotions, thoughts, and physical reaction – to ensure that your own behavior is neutral and appears unaffected by the child's behavior
4. **Disengage** before you use Value Options
   - **Strategic Praise –** praise your child for becoming calm after you disengage
   - **Parenting Empowerment** – determine your child's long-term needs, and figure out how you can help your child learn how to solve her own problems
   - **Empathy** – you've probably been in the same situation your child is in now, so you should have some understanding of your child's emotions
   - **Affection** – reach out to the child in an affectionate way

Step #3: Offer 2 options

- **Only give two options,** anymore than two and the situation will become more difficult than it has to be. **Make the options realistic for the child to achieve.** You want the child to succeed in making a decision and completing the goal.
- Part of this step is **teach the child that there are rewards and consequences for every decision,** and that it is important to think about the options before making a decision.

How do you word it?

> **Option 1: state the behavior you want to see AND the reward**
>
> **Option 2: state the behavior you DON'T want to see and emphasize that the reward doesn't come with this option**

> "Ok, here are your options: you can either clean your room tonight AND be able to play with your friends all day tomorrow. OR, you can clean your room tomorrow, and have less time to play with your friends."

In that example, the intrinsic statement is, "No matter what, you're going to have to clean your room." However, by framing it in the form of Value Options, **you're teaching that good things happen for good behaviors.**

- Make sure the options are things that you can follow-through with. You don't want to give an ultimatum that you can't follow-through with. **These are a few bad examples:**

"Ok, here are your options: you can either eat your dinner, or else."
"Ok, here are your options: you can either eat your dinner, or go to bed hungry."
"Ok, here are your options: you can either eat your dinner, or I'll feed it to you."

Obviously, it wouldn't be feasible to follow through with any of those statements. Not only are those statements unrealistic, but they also have an aggressive tone.

"Or else what?"
"Your child has to eat sometime!"
"Are you going to feed the child at every meal time?"

- **Remember, Value Options is not about gaining power as the parent.** Value Options is about getting your child to do what you need him to do.

"Ok, here are your options: eat all your dinner and you can have dessert, OR don't eat all your dinner and go without a dessert."

Step #4: Follow-through with the child's decision
- **You have to follow through with the decision,** you can't turn back. You can't offer an option that is attached to a reward, and not give the reward for the behavior. Also, you can't offer an option that is attached to a consequence, and then not follow through with the consequence. To the child, that is the same as rewarding the child for the unwanted behavior.
- **State the consequences** as you follow through to help the child knows what is happening. Use the Assertive Communication style, with the "I want," "I need," and "I feel" statements.
- **Allow the child to change her mind** – that is part of the learning process. Most of the time when the child chooses the wrong decision, she's just testing you to see if you'll really follow through. When this happens, remain calm and enforce the decision. **After all, it was the child's decision.**
- **Please remember to use** *The Calm Tone* throughout this process. You're not trying to punish the child, you're trying to teach. Anything other than a Calm Tone will shut down the process.
- **Practice makes perfect.** You're not going to get it right every time, but as you gain experience with Value Options, you'll become more proficient, and the wording for the options statements will come naturally.

Triggers & Power struggles
Notice your triggers, things that set you off, and cause you to veer off of the skills process. When you recognize a trigger, pause and then disengage. Regroup and restart the 3 Ps' with a Calm Tone. This should help to avoid having to use a discipline strategy, but if you have to, use Value Options with a Calm Tone.

Power struggles can often be a trigger for most parents. Power struggles are conflicts started by the child, with the sole purpose of gaining power or earning respect. There are several different types of power struggles:

- Passive-aggressive: characterized by passive-aggressive communication, like sarcasm and snide comments in an attempt to gain respect
- Aggressive: arguing, yelling, or physical aggression with the intent of intimidating, threatening, or scaring the other person into submissiveness
- Intellectual power struggles can look like a debate, where the child tries to "prove a point" with the intent of talking the parent into submission

Affection is pre-emptive

You never thought you'd see affection and discipline in the same chapter, but we can't stress enough how important affection is in preventing unwanted behaviors. Affection is the best way to get a child to follow you anywhere and do anything.

Getting your child to do what you want them to do sounds a lot like what a supervisor does at work. In that regard, parenting is not that different from personnel management. Affection is very similar to charisma that effective leaders use to get people to follow.

> **We can't stress enough how important affection is in preventing unwanted behaviors. Affection is the best way to get a child to follow you anywhere and do anything.**

Good leaders:

- Earn trust
- Give feedback, while maintaining relationships
- Accept feedback
- Communicate effectively
- Make good decisions
- Role model the behaviors that they want to see in their followers

Affection is a show of love or warmth that helps to develop a relationship. A common misconception is that mothers are supposed to be more affectionate than fathers, which doesn't have to be the case. Fathers can show affection in different ways, tailored to the father's personality. **Affection can be expressed in many different ways, and is often characterized by:**

- Appropriate physical contact
- Being playful
- Tender tones
- Loving remarks

Some examples of affection include:

- The high five
- Play
- Tickling
- Quiet time
- Cuddling
- Reading time
- Conversation
- Hugging
- Kissing
- Holding
- Laughing
- Unplanned praise statements

Playtime

Parents don't play with their children enough, because of the daily hustle and bustle. However, children learn through play, with parents and other kids. Play is a skill that children have to learn, and a child who hasn't learned good communication or relationship-building skills may have problems playing well with other children.

You should play with your child as often as possible, and while you're playing, be on the lookout for skills that you can teach. Playtime is a great way to proactively teach important skills.

Skills to teach during play:

- Healthy communication
- Sharing
- Friendship skills
- Problem-solving
- Respect for others
- Respect for things (toys, crayons, etc)
- Affection

You can reinforce those behaviors during play, just like you would reinforce a behavior at any other time.

The Self Esteem Myth

Topics in this chapter

What is self-esteem?

Floccinaucinihilipilification

Self-concept

Personality

Resiliency – defending the self esteem

Special issues for adolescents

Self Esteem & Our actions

The Self Esteem Myth

Self Esteem is not just "how you feel about yourself"

Self-esteem is the measure of:
- One's belief that he/she can cope
- One's belief that he/she can meet goals
- One's belief that he/she can assert his wants, needs, and values

Self-concept is based on:
- Power
- Significance
- Competence
- Values

Resiliency – the ability to cope (how we protect the self esteem) – is based on:
- Internal contribution (from self)
  - Support network (finding people to ask for help)
  - Problem-solving skills (learning how to ask for help)
  - Ability to get people to help (social skills, sense of humor, communication skills)
  - Autonomy
- External contribution (from others)
  - Acceptance
  - Participation
  - High-expectations/willingness to teach skills

Basically, self esteem is based on one's ability to meet goals and get what he/she needs.

What is self esteem?

Most people will answer that self esteem is "how I feel about myself." That is the myth. That is the popular understanding, because the real answer requires additional explanation. This chapter will not go into all of the details described by the research data, but instead will summarize those findings to provide an easy understanding of self esteem.

Some professionals can go on and on describing self esteem, and have even developed long, intricate tests to determine a person's self esteem. They can cite a myriad of research, and tell parents all of the things that they need to do in order for their children to have healthy self esteems.

Self Esteem is basically the measure of one's belief that he or she can meet goals and get what he or she needs.

There have been reports that the media affects self esteem, peers, drugs, sports, school, teachers, parents, and even a person's appearance can affect self esteem. Although these things can play a part in one's self esteem, they do not singularly define self esteem.

If a professional wanted to give a short explanation for the question, "What is self esteem," a better answer would be that:

A person's self esteem will improve as her belief in her ability to meet goals and needs improves, and will deteriorate as her belief that she can meet goals and needs deteriorates. This simple measure of one's belief in oneself can be separated into three smaller facets of self esteem:

- The measure of one's belief that he/she can cope
- The measure of one's belief that he/she can meet goals
- The measure of one's belief that he/she can assert his wants, needs, and values

The ability to cope with everyday life, often referred to as resiliency, has its own definition, which we will discuss later. Coping skills are usually learned during childhood, and require both internal and external contribution, meaning that the person has to be able do things for himself, and that other people, usually friends and family provide help, expectations, and feelings of belonging. Coping skills are the tools that we use to protect our self esteems.

The ability to meet goals is simple, and is usually measured by a person's accomplishments. The types of accomplishments can vary from person to person and culture to culture. For example, girls generally value different things than boys, and therefore goals and values will differ between girls and boys. Also, in some cultures affluence is defined by the size of one's house and the type of car in the garage. In other cultures, affluence is defined by the amount of free time that a person may have for leisure, religion, and family.

The idea that is most important to parents in helping the child develop self esteem is that the parent's role requires A LOT more than telling the child, "You're a good kid." **The parent has to help the child accomplish goals** and develop healthy relationships in order for the child to maintain his self esteem.

The ability to assert one's wants needs and values goes back to the chapter on communication. Assertive communication is generally meant to express a desire or feeling, and to have that desire or feeling supported. So the belief in one's ability to assert his wants, needs, and values, begins with his ability to communicate with others and to get others to support him.

Floccinaucinihilipilification

Floccinaucinihilipilification – the estimation of something as worthless – is a long word meaning nothing. As many "theories" as there are out there supporting the myths that surround the definition of self esteem, there is just as much research out there dispelling those myths.

A 1995 study proved no correlation between self esteem and physical attractiveness when attractiveness was judged by others, and also reported a strong correlation between self esteem and self-judged physical attractiveness, meaning that those with high-self esteem believed that they were physically attractive even though others may not have thought the same.

> The simple truth is that the person has to be able to meet goals and work on himself, in order to maintain his self esteem, in order to feel self-worth. The things that you do for yourself and others affect your self esteem, not the other way around.

Another myth is that people with high self esteem have more friends and have an easier time making friends, but a 1995 study of 542 ninth-graders found only a modest correlation. There have also been studies concerning the media's affect, puberty, and delinquency, all of which have at best only a moderate correlation with self esteem. The myth that improving one's self-esteem will improve school performance, social skills, and confidence has also been studied, and it has been found that improving those factors actually improve self esteem.

Amidst all of the myths and contradictions, we do know is that a person has to be able meet goals and work on himself, in order to maintain his self esteem, in order to feel self-worth. The things that you do for yourself and others affect your self esteem, not the other way around.

Self-concept

There are two ways that a person expresses her self esteem: self concept and personality. The self concept is a person's expression of self esteem to herself, constantly measuring who she perceives she is in comparison to who she would ideally like to be. Most people don't think of themselves in these specific terms, but often characterize their perceived selves in four particular categories.

Four ways people generally view themselves:

- **Power** – one's ability to control her environment
- **Significance** – how important one feels he is to others
- **Competence** – one's belief that she is capable of completing tasks
- **Morality** – the level at which a person is living by his value set

Power, one's confidence in her ability to control or affect her environment, can be perceived to be limited in many different ways, by parents, teachers, employers, and tough situations that can create what the person may see as 'not leaving any options.' Depression, and possibly suicide, can result when a person's situation causes him to believe that he doesn't have any options.

Parents can teach power as a skill and even use it as a tool to avoid power struggles, which can be common with small children and adolescents. It is important to teach the child that she always has complete power to make decisions for herself, and that there will always be an outcome based on the decision. It is important to teach that the outcome will usually be positive if the decision was good, but could have negative consequences if the decision is bad.

Adolescents are often in tough situations, because they are in the transitional period between childhood and adulthood. Childhood is a period when the child doesn't have to have power, because a lot of things are done for him, but may attempt to gain power in finding her roles at home and school. As he enters adulthood, he finds that he has to have power in his life roles in order to

Significance is measured in how important we feel we are to others. This is usually a measure of the strength of the relationships that are important to us.

The types of relationships that are important may vary from person to person. For example, one person may value relationships at work or with customers more than friendships outside of work, if the career track is ordered high in the person's value set. Parents usually value relationships with their kids more than any other relationship.

People who are important to us can affect our feeling of significance in both negative and positive directions. The feelings of belonging and love are great indicators that we are important in the relationship. In an unhealthy relationship, a person will tend to both maintain the relationship and try to change the things that affect his feeling of significance, or will try to remove himself from the relationship.

Some people may place value on the tangible contributions that she brings to the relationship, such as being the family breadwinner, being able to drive the kids to soccer practice or play dates, or managing the family finances. These types of contributions can provide a level of significance, as long as the person is comfortable with his roles.

When our children run into trouble, whether at school, with the law, financially, or in relationships, our measure of our own significance as parents can be affected, feeling as if we somehow let our kids down. This is a normal emotion for parents, but we have to be careful to not overcompensate for these perceived failures, and trust that we are doing the best job we can at being a good parent.

Parents can teach and reinforce significance with praise for doing good things with siblings ("Oh, you're such a good big brother. Your sister loves you so much."). Parents can also encourage their children to be helpful and mindful of others' needs, or even help develop a sense of community through volunteering, being a good neighbor, and helping with work around the house.

Competence is the confidence in one's skills – skills at work, school, in the home life, and in developing and maintaining relationships – and is more likely to change frequently compared to the other three characteristics of self concept, because it is affected by every situation that the person may be in everyday. Competence can make situational self esteem rise and fall, depending on the person's ability to use existing skills or gain new skills, problem-solve the situation, or find help.

It is relatively easy to improve competence, because children always want to learn new things. A parent cannot possibly teach everything – chemistry, philosophy, music – but a child can learn how to find answers. It is important that parents empower children to solve problems for herself, and not simply solve problems for them. The important skills to teach regarding competence include:

- Who/How to ask for help
- Common places that will help find answers to problems
- The basic problem-solving process

> **Skills to improve the self concept**
>
> Teach that the child always has decision-making power
>
> Teach that there are always outcomes to every decision, positive and/or negative
>
> Allow them to form their own opinions, but continue to teach core values
>
> Teach how to ask for help and where to look for answers to problems
>
> Teach the child that he/she can solve problems for himself/herself
>
> Help the child identify important values and teach her to live in accordance with those values
>
> **The child has to see the parent role model all of these skills!**

Morality in relation to self concept is not a person's perception of whether or not his values are good or bad, but instead it is a self-judgment of whether or not his behaviors are consistent with his values. A person's perception of her morality will be lower if she believes that she is not living according to her values, and it will be higher if she believes that she is living in accordance with her values.

For example, a person who values a healthy lifestyle, but suffers from a substance addiction, will probably have a lower perception of himself because of his morality conflict. The same would also be true for a person who values drug use and a "party lifestyle," but isn't living that lifestyle for whatever reason. In contrast, a person would have a higher self concept if she values the healthy lifestyle and is living it, or values the "party lifestyle" and is living it.

How does a person measure these traits?

People usually don't sit down and calculate their self concepts, as if they were balancing their checkbooks and planning on future events that they may need to pay for. However, make no mistake that people are constantly reassessing the self concept daily, weekly, monthly, and on those special occasions that make us think about who we are in relation to the rest of the world.

Although people don't generally go into this much detail, the easiest way to look at how a person evaluates the self concept is in a graph form. We'll put the four characteristics of self concept in bar graph form ranging from 0 (low self concept) to 10 (high self concept). We can then put our perceived self concept in red next to the ideal self concept in blue.

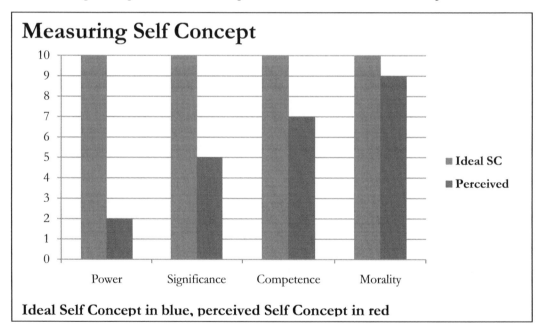

Measuring Self Concept

Ideal SC
Perceived

Power   Significance   Competence   Morality

Ideal Self Concept in blue, perceived Self Concept in red

The easiest way to measure yourself concept is by asking, on a scale of 1-10, how much power do I have in my life? How significant am I to others? How competent am I at my job and home life? Am I living by my values?

For the example above, the person is feeling almost powerless in his life, meaning that the person feels that he is unable to change or affect his situation, including the home life, school, work, or other relationships that are important to him, even though he feels competent to be able to do the things for which he is responsible. His power is rated at 2 on a scale of 10, while competence is rated at a 7 on a scale of 10.

This person also feels only somewhat significant to others, rated at 5 out of 10. There are several ways this could be interpreted, the person could feel a loss in an important relationship, or that important relationships have changed recently or even that the person feels that he is lacking relationships. Last, the person does feel confident that his actions in the different areas of his life do match his value set, rated at 9 out of 10.

Again, most people don't think about their self concept like this, but it is easy to see the areas of this person's life that are affecting his self concept. We're not saying that any one person can create the perfect life where all areas of life come out to a score of 10 out of 10 points on the self concept scale, but we will say that one the important thing to know about the self concept is that a person has to work and problem-solve her situation to at least work toward a 10 out of 10 rating.

In order to improve your own self concept, you have to be able to determine the things that you can do to increase your power, significance, competence, and morality scores. **Make realistic goals,** you don't have to turn a score of 2 into a 10 in order to improve your self esteem. Remember, the self esteem is based on achieving goals, which includes even the smallest goals. Changing a 2 to a 2.5 is a great start.

- How can you increase your power in your home and work environments?
- What can you do to improve your relationships?
- What can you do to improve your level of competence in your job, parenting skills, and other areas of your life that are important to you?
- How do your actions fit with your value set? What are your values?

The connection between self concept and self esteem is apparent.

Self Esteem	Self Concept
Confidence in ability to think and cope	Competence at work, home, and any other important function
Confidence in ability to meet goals	Power at home, work, and any other function; Perception of one's morality affects goals and changes in values
Confidence in ability to assert wants, needs, and values	Feeling of significance equates to strength of relationships; stronger relationships will help meet goals, respect wants and needs, and share common values

Personality

We could write thousands of pages on personality, based on the available research and theory. The psychology sections in books stores and libraries are filled with books on the personality, determinants, and disorders. The study of personality has even reached into business, and is taught in MBA courses, for a number of topics, including fitting an employee's personality to jobs, tasks, and companies, and conflict management using an understanding of personality traits.

Allow your child to develop his own personality; don't try to change his personality

Foster your child's personality, and trust that your child will fit into whatever future that she builds for herself. One of the toughest things that we have to do for our kids is to let them be their own persons, and to let go of the dreams that we imagined for them.

So, we won't delve into the subject here, but merely give the basics. **At its most basic level, personality is what we show others about our self esteems.** Research has shown that there is a correlation between a person's self esteem and certain personality traits, such as emotional stability and extraversion, and at least a moderate correlation to conscientiousness.

An extravert can be described as a person who uses and enjoys the world outside of herself to find spiritual energy for relationships, behaviors, and work. The extravert is often described as being sociable, easy to talk to, and directing energy and behavior outwardly, towards others or the surrounding environment, and is sometimes said to be the life of the party.

An introvert is usually described as someone who finds spiritual energy from within himself, and focuses his behaviors inward. The introvert is often described as quiet, a better listener than a talker, preferring self-reflection, and privacy, and may even be seen as shy.

The connection between self esteem and extraversion found in personality research does not suggest that your child will have a strong self esteem if she is an extravert, we don't want to simplify the subject to that extent. However, if we look at how a person evaluates and protects his self esteem, a healthy self esteem relies on some extraverted tendencies, such as asserting wants, needs, and values, asking for help, and social competence.

Also, having introverted tendencies does not guarantee that the child will have a weak self esteem. Self-reflection is a necessary part of evaluating values and goals. Introverted tendencies also include the ability to focus behaviors to complete tasks, and the ability to listen and learn, which is important for building skills and developing competence.

Foster your child's personality, and trust that your child will fit into whatever future that she builds for herself. One of the toughest things that we have to do for our kids is to let them be their own persons, and to let go of the dreams that we have for them.

Resiliency – defending the self esteem

In relation to self esteem, resiliency is the ability to cope with life events, to resist risk factors that may be harmful to the person, and the ability to bounce back from personal problems, hazards, or disasters. Resiliency is how we protect our self esteems.

Things we can do to protect our self esteems:
- Competence in social skills
- Sense of autonomy
- Develop problem-solving skills

Things we should get from others to protect our self esteems:
- Skills
- Reinforcement
- Opportunities

Internal factors for resiliency (things the child has to learn to do for herself):

Social competence

- The child has to learn social skills, and most importantly communication skills.
- The child has to learn how to get positive responses from others, which can come in the form of a smile, compliments, rewards, help, etc.
- The child has to develop a sense of humor
- The child should be able to show empathy, sympathy, and caring for others
- The child should learn flexibility and adaptability

Autonomy

- The child has to be allowed to develop a sense of autonomy, or independence
- Autonomy includes a sense of self-worth that is separate from the family unit
- The child must be able to identify and manage goals and values that may be separate from the family's goals and values
- The child should understand that she always has power to make her own decisions, but that every decision is attached to a positive or negative consequence

Problem-solving skills

- The child should be encouraged to ask for help, but that help should only be advice, and should not solve problems for the child
- The child should be able to accept "no" for an answer, but also be able to develop healthy alternatives
- The child should learn critical thinking skills, reflective thought, and ultimately abstract ideas, which are the rules and reasons behind the behaviors that we want them to exhibit

The external factors for resiliency (things others have to do for the child)

Skills

- Someone has to teach the child social and problem-solving skills, as well as where and who to go to for help
- Skills should be role modeled and reinforced by the family
- Children have to be encouraged to go to school, to prepare for college, develop career opportunities
- The parents have to role model 'Work Ethic,' the ability to get and maintain a job
- Parents should develop the sense that learning is a life-long process to embrace, not avoid

Reinforcement

- Someone important to the child must reinforce good behaviors and teach to bad behaviors. Important relationships can include parents, siblings, teachers, group leaders in other functions, like church, sports teams, or other community groups
- Reinforcement should encourage higher goals and teach abstract concepts, such as rules and reasons that make the behavior important
- Reinforcement should be focused on specific wanted behaviors with long-term effects
- Punishment should be avoided as much as possible, because it breaks down trust and communication. In instances where negative consequences are necessary, the parent should emphasize the negative reaction to the decision the child made, and not that the child is being punished.

Opportunities

- The child must be given opportunities that are important to him, even if they are not important to the parent
- Opportunities should include sports, chores, school work, and other activities that allow the child to feel significant
- Opportunities should be challenging, encouraging higher expectations, and giving the child a sense of accomplishment upon completion

Research on the risk factors that can affect the self esteem is abundant; most of the interest in risk factors has come from delinquency, drug, and relapse prevention. The things that act as risk factors exist on many different levels – the individual level, the interpersonal level, risk factors in the community, as well as societal factors. Some of these risk factors include:

- Lack of problem-solving skills
- Lack of social skills
- Lack of commitment to school or work
- Family conflict
- Lack of structure in the home environment
- History of high-risk behaviors by family members
- School failure
- Unhealthy peer relationships
- Anti-social behavior, usually learned from the family unit
- Poor or absence of relationships with family members
- Lack of community resources that could provide healthy outlets
- Neighborhood risk factors, such as access to drugs, crime, and gangs
- Socioeconomic barriers to resources

There are ways to combat these risk factors. Resiliency includes both internal factors (things that a person can do for himself) and external factors (things that other people have to do for the person) to protect the self esteem. Here, we're talking specifically about developing resiliency skills for children.

At the individual level, a person must:

- Be motivated to problem-solve
- Possess the skills to problem-solve life problems
- Be open to learn new skills and experience new things

At the interpersonal level, a person must have family, friends, and personal contacts who:

- Provide healthy, loving environments
- Teach problem-solving skills
- Help problem-solve and meet goals
- Find healthy resources for recreation, after-school activities, and developing friendships
- Role model healthy behaviors, including the ability to ask for help
- Guide the child's plans to meet goals

The community must provide:

- A safe environment, absent of the availability of drugs, crimes, and gangs
- Schools that not only foster learning, but also a sense of ownership from students to encourage attendance and motivation to learn
- Community resources that provide safe, healthy outlets for play, sports, recreation

Societal obligations include:

- Social management of opportunities, with the awareness of the risk factors specific to socioeconomic status
- Fostering opportunities for parents with histories of high-risk behaviors, to provide training, education, and work opportunities
- Developing a social awareness of the risk factors specific to socioeconomic status, because problems generally trickle into all facets of society

What is your resiliency plan for your child?

Your child can't learn the internal resiliency skills, unless you teach or role model them — it's not like people automatically know these things. What are you doing to teach resiliency?

Social competence
_____ Teach your child social skills, especially communication skills
_____ Teach your child how to ask for help, how to network with others, and to work for rewards
_____ Play, joke, and laugh with your child
_____ Talk to your child about what other people "might be thinking or feeling"
_____ Reduce your own anxiety, teach your child that there is a solution for every problem

Autonomy
_____ Empower your child, let them learn from experience
_____ Praise your child often for all of the things that he/she does right
_____ Talk to your child about values and goals
_____ Include the child in decisions about things that affect him/her
_____ Use the Empowering Conversation to teach consequences

Problem-solving skills
_____ Teach your child to accept feedback and ask for help
_____ Empower your child - use the Empowering Conversation
_____ Teach your child to accept "No" for an answer
_____ Read, play games, dream, and research the internet with your child

Special issues for adolescents

Autonomy is the ability to separate one's own values, goals, and actions from others', being one's own person. This is especially important to teenagers, who are constantly trying to separate themselves from their parents, while trying to fit in with their peers. A crucial shift occurs during adolescence. Although they may attempt to separate themselves from siblings, children generally assume the values and goals of their parents, including ideas of spirituality, scholastic achievement, and especially behavior.

Adolescents, however, are prone to partially assume the values of their peer groups. This is natural, and is not caused by low self esteem. Adolescence is a life phase of discovering relationships outside of the family unit, and peer groups are easily accessible through school, church, or other groups. **It is important that parents allow teenagers to express these new values without judgment,** and to maintain a home environment that preserves the connection to the family unit and the core values that the teen learned in childhood and will probably carry throughout life.

It is important for parents to adapt their personal communication skills to foster learning and empower the adolescent to solve his own problems, without discouraging the adolescent from asking the parent for help. Although the adolescent is driven by peer interaction, the home environment should always be a place that is safe and happy.

Self Esteem & Our actions

This workbook is based on specific skills that parents can use to immediately affect a child's behavior and ultimately improve the family's home environment and relationships. In this chapter, we described the processes that occur within a person that affect the way we view ourselves, and what we project to others through our behaviors.

A lot of traits are passed down through generations. Children who are abused will often become adults who are abusive. Parents who go to college will probably have children that go to college. The reason for this is because the actions of our parents, the people closest to us who we are supposed to trust for everything, affect our self esteems.

Children replicate their parents' behaviors, and more importantly, adjust their self concepts and personalities to manage the parent's behaviors within their own world views. A child will then adjust his own behaviors in order to meet the needs that he feels are unmet. If he feels that he is lacking power, he will behave in a way that will get power. The same is true for all of the self esteem needs.

Humans have a singular motivation: to meet needs. In meeting our needs, the prime objective is achieving a sense of self-actualization, a state of being where we are happy with ourselves and our roles in the world.

In any given situation, a child will react in a manner that she has learned, and if a positive outcome occurs, the child will continue to react in the same manner when the same situation reoccurs, until the outcome becomes negative or a better outcome can be achieved by acting differently. For example, if the child consistently gets up from the table at mealtime and wanders around the house seeking toys to play with, he will continue that behavior at every mealtime until an outcome occurs to change the child's need for the behavior.

In trying to meet needs, a person can operate at an animalistic level – continuing a behavior that gets good outcomes, and ending a behavior that gets bad outcomes.

Things parents can do for their child's self esteem

- Be a good role model – use good communication skills, problem solve life problems, and achieve goals
- Teach your child to problem solve, by working together – don't solve all of your child's problems
- Show your child how to make decisions, and teach that all decisions have consequences – both good and bad
- Teach skills, provide opportunities, and reinforce good behaviors
- Praise and reward good behaviors, use unwanted behaviors as teaching opportunities, and punish only when absolutely necessary
- Teach social competence by role modeling social competence, including humor, likeability, caring and empathy, asking for help, and interpersonal communication skills
- Allow adolescents to develop their own sense of who they are, but still foster a family environment that they will want to come home to
- Use The Empowering Conversation style when talking to an adolescent. Let him decide if he wants advice, and respect his boundaries if he doesn't.

The 3 R's & Other Life Skills

Topics in this chapter

The 3 R's

Respite, Recreation, & Relationship building

Planning for regression

Work Ethic solves a lot of problems

The 3 R's & Other Life Skills

The 3 R's of Parenting
- Respite – get a break from your child.
- Recreation – find activities to do as a family to relax, play, and have fun.
- Relationship-building – create an environment that allows you to be affectionate, while spending one-on-one time with your child.

Problem solving skills are the backbone of a healthy lifestyle

More R's of Parenting
- Regression Planning
- Reassessing your values, strengths, and needs
- Role modeling behaviors

Work Ethic is learned by seeing the parents work

Follow through with your goals and values

The 3 R's

In our busy lives, our leisure time activities usually don't have a high ranking in our value set. Usually everything else comes first – work, family, school – which is understandable.

The reason we put *respite, recreation, and relationship-building* in this book of parenting skills is because our leisure time activities are preventative health care techniques. They are similar to eating healthy foods, getting plenty of exercise and rest, and seeing your physician regularly.

The 3 R's are ways to prevent some of the unhealthy behaviors that our children sometimes do. The amount of time that you spend doing the 3 R's will reduce the amount of time that you have to spend changing your child's behaviors or using discipline techniques.

Respite, Recreation, & Relationship-building

- Respite – get a break from your child.
- Recreation – find activities to do as a family to relax, play, and have fun.
- Relationship-building – find activities that allow you to be affectionate while spending one-on-one time with your child.

Respite

Parenting is often a balance between providing for your child's needs and finding space and time for yourself. Respite can be as small as setting a boundary around your own desk or home office, or it could mean being able to have a date night with your special other. There are many ways to get a break from your child so that you can maintain some sanity, relieve some stress, and regroup yourself so that you can give 100% when the respite is over.

Ways you can ensure your child's safety, while getting a break:

- Grandparents
- Other family members
- Close friends
- Hire a babysitter
- After school activities (sports, clubs, rec centers)

- "Play dates"
- Trading time with spouse, other parent, or significant other
- Recreation activities that require little parent interaction

A lot of parents use respite time to get things done for the family, such as cleaning, laundry, or shopping. You can use the skills in this workbook to develop family roles to help perform the household tasks so that you can use your respite time more effectively.

- Use rewards for household chores
- Take the kids shopping with you
- Clean or do laundry while the kids are playing by themselves
- Ask for help

- Set up a specific room specifically for the kids
- Set up a room specifically for you to relax (no toys, games, or reasons to keep you from relaxing)

It is also important to find healthy activities to do during your respite time:

Activity type	Example	Benefits
Hobbies	Quilting, crafts, home improvement	Relaxing, fun, can develop into a rewarding experience
Sports	Gym, golf, walking	Improves health
Social	Seeing friends & family	Develops personal relationships
Relaxing	Spa, TV, email	Relaxing is a physical need
Development	Taking classes, home improvement	Personal enrichment, develops into a rewarding experience

Recreation

Recreation activities can also serve as respite care for parents, relieving stress as the kids play and have fun doing activities that they enjoy. Recreation activities can be planned or unplanned, can vary in size and budget, and can be relaxing or fast-paced. Some examples include:

- Going out for ice cream
- Going out to dinner
- Walking, biking, skating
- Going to the park
- Drawing, coloring, crafts
- Reading

- Camping, hiking, fishing
- Sports activities
- Going to the local rec center
- Going to grandma's house
- Going to the library
- Playing games

Use the things that are easily accessible. If your child enjoys puzzles or drawing, use those as regular recreation activities. Have things available for your child in a room where you won't worry about a mess. **You can easily find recreation activities that are cheap, quick, and easy.**

You can find numerous books and websites with recreation ideas that are cheap and low-maintenance.

- Check the library
- Have paper, crayons, markers available
- Use the internet to find ideas
- Ask teachers about activities
- Use local museums and sporting events

- The park is an unlimited resource
- Teens generally require more
- Help your teen buy a pass to a rec center
- Try scouting or church activities
- Teams or clubs at school
- Develop new interests

Obviously you want to ensure your child's safety, but most activities can be made safe and relaxing for the parent. It is important to use the same skills from this workbook while you're doing recreational activities.

- Choose your battles – remember, the activity is supposed to be fun so you'll want to allow your child a little more leeway than usual
- Activities can have two rewards: respite for the parent and exhaustion for the child – it's double respite!
- Enforce the rules when you have to, but use a Calm Tone and empower your child to make decisions for herself
- Reinforce that the activity is fun and encourage your child to be grateful
- Teach important friendship and play skills, such as sharing, communicating, and playing fairly
- Use recreational activities to express affection and share one-on-one time

Relationship building

We can't emphasize enough the affects of relationship building activities on reducing your stress or need to change your child's behaviors. We discussed in Chapter 6 that parenting is very similar to people management at work: the stronger the relationship, the more willing the child is to follow your directions and do the things that you want him to do.

We also discussed the importance of affection and quality one-on-one time in Chapter 6.

> The stronger the relationship, the more willing the child is to follow your directions and do the things that you want him to do.

One-on-one time can be spent with just one child or with all of your children as long as you can manage the interaction. You can do any of the recreation activities that you have available, and you can spend as much or as little time as you need with the child – as long as you make the interaction meaningful to the child.

There are many ways that you can build your relationship with your child, but they all have common characteristics:

- Have some fun!
- Meaningful interaction
- Conversation, not teaching or judging – there will always be time for teaching later
- Eliminate your negative communications, even if you have to bite your tongue!
- Be creative – meals, activities, jobs, chores can always turn into a game for the child

We're not saying that your relationship with your child will ever be perfect, or without conflict or stress. We are saying that there are ways that you can prevent some unnecessary stressors by making your present relationship stronger. Relationships are always changing, and it is your job to manage that change.

There is no way we could write out every possible opportunity for respite, every recreation activity, and every situation that you can create to build your relationship with your child. The main ideas of the 3 R's are:

- The goal should be for you to relieve stress and improve your relationship with your child
- Find healthy solutions, and teach your child that there are healthy lifestyle options. Some kids don't learn that, and in their teenage years will find unhealthy ways to meet the 3 R's for themselves, such as alcohol and drugs, gangs, bad boyfriends.
- Keep it simple, and stick with what works. If grandma is okay with you taking a nap at her house while the kids play, don't take advantage of grandma, but use that source of respite whenever possible.

Most people problem solve their needs by finding solutions that have worked in the past or by using the most immediate source of relief. However, there is a process to solving problems.

Relationship building

There are two guaranteed ways to do some relationship building with your child:

- **Eating** – for some reason, food brings people closer. An even more reliable approach is to have your child help you prepare the meals, talk to your child throughout the meal, and make it a special occasion when you can.

- **Working** – work always brings people closer, because they are working to complete a common goal for a shared reward. The rewards can be as simple as having an organized room, or the good feeling that comes from volunteering, or a wage earned from completing the job.

Planning for regression

If you learn the skills in this book and change your behaviors, you will see changes in your child's behaviors, the stress level in the home, and the interaction of the family. If you implement an action plan at school (see Chapter 9), you will probably see changes in your child at school and other important areas of her life.

Regression, going back to old behaviors, can occur – that is a normal process, so don't overreact when it occurs. The good news is that you already have implemented the *Magic Formula*, so it will be easier to readjust your child's behaviors and you will see results sooner.

Values and goals are always changing, so you will first need to reassess any new goals that you could implement with your child. Parenting is a process – the values, goals, and rewards may change, but the skills that you will use – The Calm Tone, Effective Reinforcement, and Parenting Empowerment – will always stay the same.

Also, the child has already "bought into" the reward process, and understands that certain behaviors will get rewards. The only changes that you may need to make at this point is to focus on new goals with new rewards, emphasizing to the child that you still expect to see the behaviors that you've already established.

The ABC's of Problem-Solving

Assess: assess the situation, your values, and your needs. Make sure that your decision is consistent with your values and goals.

Brainstorm: for possible solutions, consider the pro's and con's of each possible solution.

> There are many ways to brainstorm, but the easiest way is to make a list of possible solutions, and then work through your list, eliminating options due to the negative consequences that could come from the decision.

Consult – ask for help, if you need it! There is always someone who can help!

> Being able to get people to help you is important to your self esteem – which can affect some of the stressful symptoms that you may be experiencing, such as anxiety, powerlessness, and depression.

Decide – choose an option. Act on that decision, and give it 100% effort. Make sure that YOU make the decision, take the power over your situation.

Evaluate the outcome and make any needed changes. Tweak your plan of action, and communicate to others that your plan is changing.

You may regress, going back to some of your old parenting skills – Negative Communication skills, Ineffective Discipline techniques, Enabling – and you may not realize that the change in your child's behavior could be a result of your regression.

Develop a family system for managing goals
- **Be able to accept feedback,** even from your child. This is one of those behaviors that extends beyond the home, into school, work, and other relationships, so it is important that you role model this skill to your child.

  There is no better way to role model Accepting Feedback than while you are trying to evaluate the family's values, your child's goals, and your needs from the child. Include your child in on the conversation, and you will probably find that your child has her own goals, like learning to skateboard or starting karate.
- **Communication is critical.**   It is okay for your child to assert his wants, needs, and values, and most of the time, his values will be similar to yours. Talk to your child about your expectations, "Hey, I'd like to work on using a Calm Tone at school. You're very good at it when you're at home with me, but you seem to get into trouble for yelling and arguing at school."
- **Keep replacing the carrot.** Once you reward your child for accomplishing goals or changing the behaviors that you targeted, find a new goal that will be attached to a new

reward. Keep the goals slightly beyond your child's capabilities, so that she has to work for the reward.

The reinforcement system that you have established will not change, even when you increase your expectations of your child. Your child will always want Strategic Praise and the other rewards that you have implemented in your home.

<u>Role model target behaviors</u>
We discussed earlier the need to role model behaviors, to let your child SEE what is expected. You have to use The Calm Tone in order for your child to see what it looks and sounds like. You have to use good communication skills in order to expect your child to use good communication skills.

This book discusses the skills that form a working home environment, but the child will emulate the skills at school, work, and in other relationships if you are role modeling those skills. Other skills that you will want to role model include:

- Physical health – having a healthy lifestyle, reducing health risks
- Accountability – taking responsibility for your actions
- Honesty – dealing with people honestly, without manipulation or deceit
- Problem solving – being able to find solutions and ask for help
- Maintaining healthy friendships – keeping personal relationships beyond the family
- Academic success – being successful at school and building skills
- Financial stability – being able to provide for yourself and your family
- Work Ethic – getting your job done as good as possible

When regression occurs…

1. Don't panic, it's going to happen.
2. Check your Value Set and goals, and do the same for your child. Values and goals are always changing; reassess your family's strengths and needs.
3. Hone your skills – go back through this workbook for a refresher. Make sure that you are confident with your skills:
   - The Calm Tone
   - Disengaging
   - Effective Reinforcement
   - Parenting Empowerment
4. Problem-solve… the problem behaviors may only be short-term issues where the child is testing new boundaries.
5. Remember your 3 R's – they act as preventative tools and stress relief
6. Ask for help! Use your network; call a friend, your physician, your old therapist.

Work Ethic solves a lot of problems

Work Ethic is the ability to get a job done quickly, cheaply, and as good as possible. That is what employers expect from employees. There are other characteristics of Work Ethic that are also important:

- Organization & Time Management

- Punctuality
- Professionalism
- Meeting goals
- Effective communication skills

Work Ethic is learned from the parents, by seeing the work habits of the parents. **Parents who go to work every day, maintain a job, and make significant contributions to their workplace and their own careers are likely to have children who have the same habits.**

Work Ethic extends beyond the job site:
- The organization and cleanliness of your home
- Academic achievement
- Organization and stability of relationships and personal needsFinancial strength
- Career planning

Work Ethic is a contributing factor to school success and preventing delinquency. Kids with meaningful goals and have parents who have high expectations and empower them to strive for higher goals, are more likely to avoid the risk factors of everyday life. Teens are very susceptible to numerous risk factors everyday:

- Peer pressure
- Drugs and alcohol
- Lack of healthy resources
- Enabling parents

- Ineffective communication skills
- Impulsive behavior
- Irresponsive to rewards
- Lack of problem solving skills

Work Ethic provides the desire to learn new skills to overcome those risk factors, and isn't something that can be taught. It has to be role modeled by the parent. Role modeling can include physically sitting down with your child to show how to do certain things tied to Work Ethic:

- Clean the house with your child
- Show him how to create and manage a budget
- Show him how to make financial goals for something that she will want in the future
- Help him plan his educational goals, including preparing for college
- Help him plan his career goals, to start developing work skills early

The "Clean House" Exercise

Some parents think that having kids means "free labor," an attitude that can backfire by causing additional stress and conflict.

Scene: Mom tells Jen, age 16, to have the house clean by the time she gets home from work. When Mom gets home, Jen hadn't done any chores.

> Mom: Why didn't you do your chores?
> Jen: I was on the phone with Cassie, I'll do them in a little while.
> Mom: No, I told you to have them done by the time I get home from work!
> Jen: Why are you making such a big fuss? I told you I'll do them in a little while!
> Mom (yelling): No, you'll do them right now!
> Jen (yelling): No, you do them yourself!
> [Jen storms off to her room and slams the door. Mom ends up doing the chores.]

Having kids doesn't mean free labor, but parents will often try to reason that the child should do the chores because:
> "You're living in my house, so you have to contribute."
> "Because I said so."
> "Because you don't pay rent."

The situation above, where the conflict escalated rapidly indicates several things:

- A poor relationship – mom doesn't have the relationship with Jen that provides Jen with a desire to WANT to do what Mom expects
- An ineffective reinforcement system – Mom has to find other rewards that are available that Jen will find meaningful.
- Poor communication skills – Both Mom and Jen failed to use The Calm Tone, Disengaging, and Assertive Communication.
- An enabling parent – after all, Mom did end up doing the chores for Jen.

More importantly, Mom isn't really role modeling Work Ethic. Sure, she goes to work everyday, but she is role modeling the attitude that if an adult has kids and goes to work, then that adult doesn't have to do anything at home.

To effectively role model work ethic at home, Mom has to initiate the chores at home, and create an environment where Jen will WANT to help, by making the chores fun with music, playing, or conversation.

Chapter 8 - The 3 R's & Other Life Skills

Using the Network

Topics in this chapter

Who is in your network?

You get more bees with honey…

The School

Using the Network

A network is a collection of people, services, and other resources that you can use to get help for yourself and your child

Use your network to help implement the behavior changes that you are trying to make at home

The Family has a Self Esteem – and it is your job to protect it

Develop problem solving skills and use The Calm Tone when working with your network

The school can be a great help in reinforcing the behaviors that you are teaching at home – ask for help from teachers and administrators.

Detail Focus Skills are a great way for improving your child's homework experience and reducing your home-work time stress

Who is in YOUR network?

A network is a collection of people, services, and other resources that you can use to get help for yourself and your child. Some examples of people in your network can include:

- Extended family
- Your friends
- Older children
- The school
- Church programs
- After school clubs
- Sports teams
- Government agencies
- Doctors & Therapists
- Community agencies

The Family Self Esteem

Your family has a self esteem that is based on the sum of each member's self esteem. When one person in the family is experiencing a period of lower self esteem or self concept, then the entire family will experience the same drop in self esteem.

The family also has the ability to protect its self esteem – family resiliency – using the same skills that individuals must use to be resilient. Family resiliency depends on both the strength of individual members, as well as the synergy between the family members.

The Victim role is characterized by:
- Using "should" statements, "That person should do something for me, because..."
- Believing that you shouldn't have to ask for help, help should be automatic
- Blaming other people for your situation
- Expecting people to give you things, with nothing in return
- Asking people to show pity for you, instead of empathy or solutions
- Making excuses for your situation, rather than changing your situation

The victim role is okay – when you're alone and feeling anxious or nervous – **but will hinder your ability to improve your situation** if you are more focused on being a victim rather than finding solutions. Playing the victim role, instead of finding solutions, is a disservice to your child, and is a bad parenting and interpersonal technique.

It is okay to ask for help – that is the alternative emotion to being the victim. Asking for help is a skill that parents have to teach during the childhood stage of development. Some people don't learn that skill, and usually have problems in school and work.

It is also okay to not know answers, but it is not okay to lie about knowing an answer or not solving problems that affect your child. It is important to note that it is important for you to empower your child to solve his own problems, but here we are talking about your child's behavior problems that you are trying to change.

Don't abuse your network, because you never know when you may need it again. Use good communication skills when you go to your network for help, and be able to accept "NO" for an answer. If one person in your network can't help you, be okay with that, and move on to the next person. Also, don't overuse your network, do as much of the work as possible in implementing solutions.

Finally, take power over your situation – YOU SOLVE YOUR PROBLEMS.

Using the Network

Problem solving is very important for the family to use the network efficiently to produce the best short-term and long-term solutions. There are several factors that are especially important:

- Don't be the victim, be the person looking for options
- Ask for help
- It is okay to not know the answer to a problem; it is not okay to not solve problems that are affecting your child
- Don't abuse your network
- Give back to your network
- **Most importantly: IT IS YOUR JOB TO FIND ANSWERS, BUT YOUR NETWORK CAN HELP**

You get more bees with honey...

Use the ABC's of problem solving to help you brainstorm before you contact your network. Assess your problem and the possible ways that your network could help. Sit down and make a list of all of the possible solutions that you could implement, and determine whether or not they fit your value set.

Once you complete your own brainstorming session, you can begin consulting with people in your network. **Your communication skills are critical when you're using your network resources** to help you find answers and implement solutions. The last thing you want to do is agitate a resource that you may need in the future.

First, you'll get people to *want* to help you if you're nice about it. Second, it is easier to find solutions when you already have a starting place. You may have to bounce from person to person within your network as you brainstorm for solutions, before finally coming up with the answer to your problem, so be patient. Third, don't settle the most immediate answer or the easiest option, if that solution doesn't fit your values and goals.

When you make your decision, follow through with your commitments to your network. More importantly, follow up with your network resources to make sure they are doing what they said they are going to do.

This includes:

- Making sure that teachers follow through with rewards and consequences
- Determining the needs of your spouse or other parent
- Ensuring that your spouse or other parent is keeping the same values and goals
- Calling your contacts at the various agencies to make sure they followed through with their commitments
- Calling friends and extended family for respite

The ABC's of Problem-Solving

Assess: assess the situation, your values, and your needs. Make sure that your decision is consistent with your values and goals.

Brainstorm: for possible solutions, consider the pro's and con's of each possible solution.

There are many ways to brainstorm, but the easiest way is to make a list of possible solutions, and then work through your list, eliminating options due to the negative consequences that could come from the decision.

Consult – ask for help, if you need it! There is always someone who can help!

Being able to get people to help you is important to your self esteem – which can affect some of the stressful symptoms that you may be experiencing, such as anxiety, powerlessness, and depression.

Decide – choose an option. Act on that decision, and give it 100% effort. Make sure that YOU make the decision, take the power over your situation.

Evaluate the outcome and make any needed changes. Tweak your plan of action, and communicate to others that your plan is changing.

The School

The school can be a tough place to navigate, sometimes presenting barriers that make it difficult for parents to engage in the problem solving process. Most school problems can be solved by the teacher in the classroom without having to communicate with the parent. Minor problems can include:

- The child being too talkative
- The child not following instructions
- Talking out of turn
- Not getting along with classmates

We are not concerned with the minor problems – those things happen. Our intent in this chapter is to discuss escalated problems at school:

- Persistent problems (such as being talkative, even after receiving a consequence)
- Oppositional Defiance Disorder
- Conduct Disorder
- Excessive truancy
- Persistent school failure (such as constantly being removed from class, consistent relationship problems, and defiance of rules)

Kids are very good at problem solving situations, and will find ways to meet their needs, including getting things that they want, as well as relieving fear, anxiety, or any other aversive situation.

Some of the common aversive situations that a child encounters in school include:

- Bullying
- Reading anxiety
- Math anxiety
- Performance anxiety
- Peer pressure that clashes with family values
- Problems on the bus
- Socioeconomic symptoms: tattered or worn clothing, lack of school supplies, malnutrition, etc.
- Adolescent girls may have anxieties surrounding gym class (not wanting to dress out), relationship problems (especially with boyfriends), and issues with menstruation

Eliminating barriers to learning

There are always reasons for behaviors, which means that there are always solutions to change behaviors. Here are the most common problems that we have seen:

Reading anxiety is a common cause of persistent school failure and persistent behavior problems. Reading anxiety usually occurs when the child recognizes that he does not perform at the same level as his peers, and can become embarrassed. More severe cases may purposely misbehave in order to be removed from class, so that they don't expose their own feelings of inferiority.

Performance anxiety, including in class activities, test anxiety and oral presentations, may or may not be linked to a learning disorder, meaning that it can occur regardless of academic strength. Behavior problems due to reading or performance anxieties can be common for middle and high school students – adolescents concerned with acceptance from peers. Being kicked out of class is a reward to some kids, because it removes anxiety and gives them a status among peers.

Enabling parents, which we discussed in Chapter 5, can also contribute to poor school performance in a number of ways:

- By not managing homework time effectively.
- By "swooping in" when the child has behavior problems, not allowing teachers to give consequences for actions
- By making excuses for the child's truancy or inability to turn in school work

Bullies and peer pressure can cause a child to act out in class, in the lunchroom, on the bus, and anywhere else where there may be limited adult supervision. A child who feels scared or nervous because of the potential of being bullied may act out to avoid the aggressor or strike first. To address bullying:

- Notify the school administration of supervision problems
- Teach your child healthy ways to avoid or address aggressors
- Teach your child to manage her environment (sit in the front of the class, sit near non-threatening people, eat lunch with friends, sit at the front of the bus)

Getting people to help you

1. **Use The Calm Tone**: there may be times when someone in your network pushes your buttons, especially if you have to wait in line at a government agency just for the person at the desk to tell you that you waited in the wrong line.

   The Calm Tone is very important in those situations; **most people are more willing to help people who are calm and polite, rather than aggressive or pushy.** Also, most people work better in less stressful situations.

2. **Be assertive**: start your sentences with "I want," "I need," or "I feel." Protect your values and goals as you brainstorm for solutions.

3. **Have solutions in mind**: do your own brainstorming before you go to your network. You can often use your network to build upon your own ideas until you find the optimal solution.

   Also, brainstorming before you contact your network will help you shape your boundaries – what you're willing to do and not do. You will be showing your resources that you've already started the work, and that you need help.

4. **Be persistent** – go after what you want, and communicate with your resources regularly and often. Ask a lot of questions to get a good picture of what you're dealing with and what it's going to take to implement your solution.

5. **Follow through** – do what you say you're going to do, and then evaluate later. Your network is less likely to help in the future if you don't follow through with your own responsibilities.

6. **Follow up**: contact your network to make sure that they are following through with what they said they will do. Make sure that they are maintaining your plan.

Meeting your child's physical needs is critical to academic success, and there are ways to provide food, clothing, and school supplies, even on a limited income.

- Feed a healthy breakfast – most schools even offer a free breakfast, lunch, and milk program for high-risk children
- Find durable, trendy clothing – there are so many brands out there these days that you can easily find something that your child will like and also fit your price range

- Make sure your child has the school supplies that are required, even if you have to approach a church or community organization

Solutions that you can implement for behavior problems at school should include:
- Reinforcing good behavior at home
- Using The Calm Tone, Effective Reinforcement, and Parenting Empowerment for homework sessions
- Reading with your child, and have your child read to you
- Creating homework sessions to emulate the classroom setting
- Developing a healthy relationship with teachers and administrative staff
- Reinforcing healthy behaviors at school and working with teachers to do the same
- Teaching to unwanted school behaviors

Solutions that you should ask the teachers to implement:
- Changing the reinforcement system – some teachers don't use reinforcement effectively
- One-on-one tutoring, especially for reading
- Keeping your child in the most normalized environment, but still allowing Effective Reinforcement and natural consequences
- Work with your therapist to implement Effective Reinforcement in the classroom
- Testing to determine academic needs
- Addressing academic needs, possibly by working with a specialist

Addressing unwanted school behaviors is very similar to addressing unwanted behaviors at home: target specific unwanted behaviors and reinforce the good behaviors. The primary difference is that you will also have to eliminate learning barriers, such as reading and performance anxieties, any enabling behaviors that *you* may be doing, and bullies.

First we should recall some vital information concerning behavior: people do things to meet needs.

Special Education issues

It is important to note that in this section, we are only discussing children with behavior-related special education needs. Parents of children with behavior problems who have learning disabilities can use the skills in this workbook effectively, but should also note that other issues may be affecting the behaviors.

By law, special education resources are supposed to be structured to provide the student with the least restrictive setting, consequences, and learning environment. Special education services are supposed to be as "normalized" as possible, meaning that students are supposed to be given services so that they "appear" just like all the other students, but still get the specialized care.

However, what schools don't tell you is that if your child's behaviors are bad enough, they will try to convince you that the most normalized setting for your child will be to separate him, put him into a class with other kids with behavior problems, and label your child as "a trouble maker."

Your job as the parent is to work with the school to get them to implement and support the same reinforcement structure that you're creating at home. In doing this, be specific about the exact behavior goals that you're working on at home.

You can use the Individualized Education Program (IEP) to help you implement your strategy. The IEP is a contract that binds the school to adhere to the strategy that is described in the IEP, which has to be developed in partnership with the parent. Ask your therapist to help you develop the behavior strategy and attend the IEP meeting.

Parents of students with disabilities

It is important to emphasize that parents of students with disabilities have to empower their child, just like every other parent. It can be very easy at times for parents to enable their special-needs child, believing that their child is more fragile because of the disability, which is certainly not the case!

The IEP should also address additional educational needs, such as allowing your child to not read out loud or give presentations if she has a reading or performance anxiety. Don't be afraid to address behavior concerns in the IEP. Tell the teachers which behaviors you are working on at home and the reinforcements that you're using to reward the targeted behaviors, and write them into the IEP:

- The Calm Tone
- Practicing calm
- Listening skills
- Being patient
- Completing tasks
- Accepting "NO"
- Eliminating argument
- Eliminating debates

- Eliminating the power struggle
- Empowering self
- Impulse control
- Delayed gratification
- Managing the environment
- Organization skills
- Detail focus

Remember, teachers have a classroom full of kids, so your child is going to be given attention equal to everyone else. There are times when a teacher may not realize that he or she must reward your child for a specific behavior – teachers are only human. In most cases, however, **you will find that teachers *are* willing to implement ideas that will work, if it will help them manage the classroom effectively.**

Once you begin the Top 3 skills at home – The Calm Tone, Effective Reinforcement, and Parenting Empowerment – you should try to keep your child in the most normalized classroom setting. This means that you should try to keep your child in the regular classroom, not in a classroom specifically for behavior problems.

Your school responsibilities

Make no mistake, the school is only responsible for half of your child's school achievement – you do have to continue the work at home. That includes modifying your parenting behavior to change the child's behaviors, but also creating a work environment at home modeled after the classroom setting.

Create a homework station:
- Lighting is very important

- Accessibility – make the station accessible to the child and within sight of the parent, to be able to monitor your child from a distance if needed.
- Keep tools in reach. Make sure your child has paper, pencils, and any other necessary school supply at the station, so that he doesn't have to leave his seat to find them.
- Remove potential distractions, such as toys, the TV, siblings, or anything else that could create an excuse to move about.
- Make the station as easy to use as possible – remove clutter, ensure ample workspace, and make it look like a fun place.

Have your child read to you to alleviate reading anxiety
- Encourage your child with Strategic Praise, even for the smallest successes
- Make reading fun! Have the child read something that she will want to read, and make sure it's not too difficult. Keep ample reading materials around the house.
- Have your child read instructions for himself, including instructions for other subjects, like math, history, or science homework. When your child begins to be frustrated with the instructions, have him reread them, and then help him without doing it for him
- Don't force anything – if your child senses your anxiety or any emotion other than happiness that she is reading, she will shut down
- Have your child read out loud to you, use Strategic Praise to reinforce that they are reading out loud
- Use the Poker Face when your child is reading, and reinforce him for trying to sound out words. Some parents and teachers don't use the Poker Face, and the child will try to guess at the words on the page, instead of sounding out the words.

Detail Focus
An important skill that most parents overlook is "Detailed Focus Skills," teaching the child to pay attention to detail to complete complex chores, tasks, and homework. Detail Focus emphasizes skills needed to complete more complicated tasks requiring delayed gratification, increased patience, and self-discipline. **This skill also teaches the child to follow instructions, and can be transferred easily to teachers.**

Initially, the skill development will require the parent's one-on-one support and reinforcement from the parent., but the goal is to increase the child's ability to work without the parent and stay with a task without taking breaks, or to be able to come back to that task with independent motivation and follow through, gradually removing your involvement.

> **Being kicked out of class is a reward to some kids, because it removes anxiety and gives them a status among peers.**

1. The target behavior is to have your child sit through a task until completion, but plan to implement this skill just as you would any other skill that you are trying to teach your child.
    - To begin you need a small task, any task – homework is an ideal task for Detailed Focus - and you can even create your own to begin to practice and develop this skill in your child.
    - Prepare reinforcement options to use after the child completes the task.
    - Use the 3 P's.
    - Set a specific and consistent time and place to complete the task.
    - Remove distractions.

2. Start with the child's challenge level on the task.
   - Stay with them to reinforce follow through with your monitoring and support.
   - Push to their level of discomfort, then break, do something easy, ideally related to the task completion, like page numbering, organizing colors, something that takes a break from the frustration area while completing the overall task.
3. Reinforce "Following Instructions."
   - Be a teacher, not a parent.
   - Be clear and use The Calm Tone.
4. Continue pushing in a supportive manner to the challenge point of frustration for the child.
   - Continue with the breaks and use Strategic Praise to emphasize their new skill development, "You are getting so much better at finishing these harder projects on your own," etc.
   - Add the reinforcement effectively with the Strategic Praise.
5. "Up the ante" – reinforce the child sitting through the task until completion.
   - Add the option for the child to delay the gratification or receipt of the reinforcement stating that you will double, triple or even quadruple the reinforcement if they complete that extra amount during that same sitting or if they choose to wait and save their reinforcement.
   - Keep a positive focus without criticizing or correcting. **A negative experience will cause the child will return to the old habit of giving up.**
   - In the beginning the child will not be good at this skill, so keep your standards lower in the beginning, gradually raising the bar as the child buys into the benefits of good, hard work and their positive pay offs.

This task is essential for children, who struggle with homework, or with turning it in, or asking question or completing research to increase grades. It is also an integral skill for successful career and relationship development. With the new technology age we have been significantly encouraged to multi-task. Without this skill the child could develop an increasing lack of patience with tasks and self-motivation through difficult or boring aspects of tasks, or even with the less interesting qualities of relationships.

As the skill develops, you can add more tasks, diverse and spontaneous reinforcers, unplanned times and places, with success.

Detail Focus Skill

This skill teaches your child to patiently work through a task until completion, and it also reduces your need to spend more time than necessary explaining tasks. It is ideal for homework time or any other task that occurs regularly.

1. The target behavior is to have your child sit through a task until completion, but plan to implement this skill just as you would any other skill that you are trying to teach your child.
2. Start with the child's challenge level on the task.
3. Reinforce "Following Instructions."
4. Continue pushing in a supportive manner to the challenge point of frustration for the child.
5. "Up the ante" – reinforce the child sitting through the task until completion.

24450686R00069

Made in the USA
Lexington, KY
19 July 2013